The "C" Planes
U.S. Cargo Aircraft: 1925- To The Present

Bill Holder
&
Scott Vadnais

Schiffer Military/Aviation History
Atglen, PA

Book Design by Ian Robertson.

Printed in China.
ISBN: 0-88740-912-1

We are interested in hearing from authors with book ideas on related topics.

Published by Schiffer Publishing Ltd.
77 Lower Valley Road
Atglen, PA 19310
Please write for a free catalog.
This book may be purchased from the publisher.
Please include $2.95 postage.
Try your bookstore first.

INTRODUCTION

For those that follow the history of military aviation through the years, it's the letters that bring out the attention.

Without doubt, the letters P and later F, for fighter and pursuit aircraft, have been the "glamour" letters. Next comes the letter B, which of course stands for bomber, and that letter also brings charisma to the designation.

Then, there is the letter C, which in terms of total number of aircraft types through the years, has seen just as many over-all systems, almost 200 in all. But mention cargo or transport aircraft, which the C designation identifies, and the connotation isn't that exciting to say the least.

Quite frankly, it comes off as a hauler, a carrier, along with the expected point-A-to-point-B machine. There are normally no offensive capabilities associated with these machines, just the transporting of material or troops to a required position. You normally don't associate these C planes with nose art, or aircraft kill markings. But you might be surprised what all the third letter designation has indicated through the years.

Missions

Well, we're here to tell you that is one large misconception for the aircraft that carry the letter C as their letter designation.

These planes through the decades represent a lot more than the cargo hauling mission. The missions besides the expected are almost too numerous to mention. Here are but a few of the "other" missions:

— Refueling
— Reconnaissance
— Electronic Surveillance
— R&D testbeds
— Gunships
— VIP/Presidential Aircraft
— Instrument Training
— Air Ambulances
— Paratrooper Carriers
— Glider Tugs
— Navigation Trainers
— Air Evacuation
— Weather Aircraft
— Hurricane Hunters
— Fuel Ferrying
— Prototype Aircraft
— Rescue Aircraft
— Assault Transports
— Ski Operations
— Drone-launching
— Fire Fighting
— Satellite Recovery
— ICBM Carriers
— Flying Command Posts
— Border Patrol

In order to identify that a C plane had an additional mission, besides the expected hauling, many times there would be a letter in addition to the C — ie. HC-130, AC-130, KC-135 etc.

But there are other additional letters, in addition to the C, that indicate its status of development. The U prefix referred to the carrying capability of the particular aircraft, in this case, a capacity of one and one-half tons, or a passenger capability of less than ten passengers.

YC and XC were designations given to the planes during phases of their development.

The YC designation was used to designate a limited production run for purposes of testing. The XC designation, which obviously stood for experimental, applied to aircraft which would be in a test status before the initiation of series production. It's interesting to note that both the YC and XC designations are still in place in the 1990s, many decades since they first came on the scene.

During the 1930s, at least three transport developments received XC designations but the numbering of these systems was completely out of bounds with the established numbering.

The systems included the XC-910 (a Boeing monomail aircraft), the XC-918 (a Douglas Amphibian), and the XC-928 (a Fairchild development). The exact meaning of these high numbered systems, which didn't align with the low two-digit C numbering of that 1930s time period, is not known.

History

Although the C designation has long been the standard designation for this type of plane, it didn't start out that way. These planes were initially designated by the letter T, and there would be three planes given that designation (T-1,2,3) in the 1920s. None would be serially produced with the T-3 being canceled in favor of the initial C-1 aircraft.

Evolution

Just as diverse as the number of missions the C planes perform, and have performed in the past, are the way the planes evolved. If you think they all followed the normal design phase going through a design, prototype, flight test, and production program, think again. It just didn't happen that way that often.

A large number of the C planes actually began life as other types of aircraft and then were converted to the C mission. In fact, the first C-designated aircraft, the Douglas C-1 was such a modification being derived from the existing O-2C Observation Plane. Other times, new C aircraft were created with improved powerplants replacing those on earlier C planes. In another interesting example of improvement to an existing C plane, the C-23 became the C-25 with the substitution of a metal fuselage. There were also bombers that would modified into C planes, an example being the C-58 which was derived from the B-18A bomber. It also happened during World War II when a cargo version of the B-24 (the C-87) was derived. There was also a fuel carrying version, the C-109, that evolved from the B-24 lineage. Probably the largest plane to experience this bomber-to-transport transformation was the XC-99 which was the cargo version of the giant B-36. During World War II, commercial-type aircraft were actually commandeered by the military for their use. One example was the so-called C-52 which was used for airborne operations.

Following World War II, in an interesting negotiation, there were some C planes (one example was the C-69) that were declared excess and sold to the airlines for their use. Amazingly, in the 1980s, the reverse procedure occurred when the Air Force bought several old Boeing 707 transports from American Airlines and converted them into C-135 flying testbeds.

There was also a C plane that received a new designation when it was converted to an Air Force One Presidential aircraft — ie. a C-135 into the VC-137. There was also one particular C-118 that was converted to the "Independence", the plane used by President Truman, although the version didn't receive a new C designation.

Maybe the best-known transport modification was the Gunship. The C-47, C-119, and C-130 all received offensive capabilities, and all saw plenty of combat.

There are other transport aircraft still receiving major improvements after many years of production, a prime example being the C-141 Starlifter. This plane was taken back to the production plant and had its fuselage stretched, along with the addition of a refueling probe. It was just like a new plane, but also did not receive a new designation, simply changing from the C-141A to the C-141B — times change, as earlier it would have probably received a new C number.

Design and Development

As was stated earlier, there are many ways the C planes have evolved through the years. As was the case with many bombers and fighter development programs, there were many than didn't make it to operational service.

There were also many transports that didn't progress beyond the drawing board stage, while others were mocked up before being canceled. Of course, many of these programs were terminated after losing in a competition with aircraft from other companies.

During the war years, with the obvious need for many of these aircraft, many of the design and development phases were speeded up, and in some cases there were no prototypes built, and the planes were rushed into production.

Characteristics

Cargo planes through the decades have varied about as much as you can imagine. The designation has appeared on tiny single engine planes which appear unable to carry anything of note, to the giant XC-99 and C-5 capable of transporting many tons of cargo thousands of miles. The evolution of size through the years is just amazing.

The wingspan of the first C aircraft, the C-1, which was first produced in 1925 had a wingspan of about 57 feet. Contrast that to the giant C-5A where the wingspan stretches 160 feet, more than half the length of a football field. The payload of the initial C-1 was a minimal 2,500 pounds, while the C-5 hauls some 255,000 pounds!

There are many planes that received the C designation. Over the years, there have been C planes with one, two, three, four, and ten engines. There was simply no template for a plane to receive this designation.

The C Numbering System

With the exception of the first T designations, cargo aircraft have always carried the C designation. But interestingly, when the official list reached the C-142 in the early 1960s (it started in the mid-1920s), the list was terminated and started over. An interesting footnote is that there was actually a C-143 given for another development, but the program would never be approved. As of printing time, the list has reached into the C-30s with no end in sight.

The Future

What will it hold for the C planes? The future appears to be unlimited. The keynote, though, is the increasing size of the projected future C planes. Some of the concepts which have been proposed are truly amazing. Whether any of them will ever be built in these hard economic times for the military remains to be seen. Undoubtedly, there will be other future C planes that will evolve as modifications to existing aircraft. It's happened before and could well repeat itself.

C-1 (No Nickname)

Manufacturer: Douglas
Production period/total: 1925-1927/27 built
Status: Operational

Serial numbers:
25-425 through 434
26-421 through 427
27-203 through 212

Variants:
C-1A: A single prototype (25-426) was re-engined with a supercharged V-1650 powerplant.
C-1B: A designation which was reserved for a variant which was never built.
C-1C: A seven passenger version of the C-1 which incorporated a three and one-half foot increase. Seventeen were built.

Statistics:
Crew: 1
Cruising speed: 100 mph
Ceiling: 16,000 feet
Range: 750 miles

Physical Characteristics:
Wingspan: 57 feet
Length: 36 feet
Height: 14 feet
Empty weight: 3,900 pounds
Gross weight: 7,400 pounds
Maximum payload: 2,500 pounds (6 to 8 passengers)

The Story
Even though the C-1 was the first aircraft to receive the C designation, there also were other factors that gave this aircraft extra prominence.

It had a dual first, being not only the first cargo aircraft but also the first personnel aircraft. And, although the C-1 was not designed for a third mission, it served as the tanker for the first-ever air-to-air refueling mission which took place in 1928. The C-1 was the Army Air Corp's standard transport until 1929.

To push the over 3.5 ton aircraft through the air, the C-1 was powered by a 400 horsepower Liberty "12" powerplant. A flight test at the time showed that the plane was capable of about 75 miles per hour. Its landing speed was about 55 miles per hour.

The plane carried about 121 gallons of fuel which accounted for less than 20 percent of its empty weight. The wing loading was eight pounds per square feet.

Surprisingly, the plane was not designed from scratch, but instead was a modification of an existing aircraft, the O-2C Observation Plane.

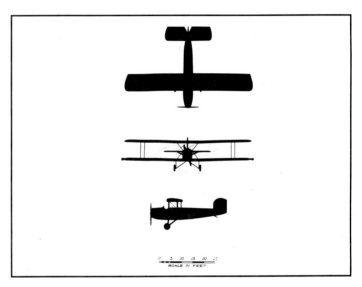

C-2 (No Nickname)

Manufacturer: Atlantic Aviation Co.
Status: Research
Production period/total: 1926-1928/11 built

Serial numbers:
26-202 through 204
28-119 through 126

Variants:
XC-2: Modifications made to 26-203.
C-2A: 28-119 through 28-126 carried this designation and had a bigger 74 foot wing.
C-7: The final variant of the C-2 was the C-7. Four of these were converted from the C-2s.

Statistics:
Crew: 2
Cruising speed: 100 mph
Ceiling: 12,500 feet
Range: 355 miles

Physical Characteristics:
Wingspan: 71 feet

Length: 48 feet
Height: 12.5 feet
Empty weight: 5,380 pounds
Gross weight: 9,175 pounds
Maximum payload: 2,000 pounds (10 passengers)

The Story
The C-2 carried the company designation of Atlantic Model 7 which was a version of the Fokker F VIIA/3m. Atlantic was actually an affiliate of the Fokker company.

The major difference in the two models was that the C-2 had a larger powerplant with an impressive trio of 225 horsepower R-790-1 engines. In addition, the C-2s also sported a larger fuselage than the Fokker configuration along with a redesigned flight deck.

The first three C-2s were delivered to the USAAC, with the first pair serving as flight test vehicles at the McCook Field complex. They were designated as P463 and P483 for this purpose.

From a publicity point of view, the C-2 showed the way with two significant accomplishments. First, it made the first trans-Pacific Ocean flight from Oakland, California to Honolulu. Later, in 1929, a C-2 (coined the 'Question Mark') established a world endurance record for remaining aloft for six days. The pilots of that flight included two (Ira Eaker and Carl Spaatz) who would later become generals in the Army Air Corps and be significant players during the World War II air war.

C-3 "Tin Goose"

Manufacturer: Stout, The Aircraft Division of Ford Motor Co.
Status: Operational
Production period/total: 1928-1929/8 built

Serial Numbers:
28-348
29-220 through 226

Variants:
XC-3: Was the prototype for the C-3. The commercial model of the model (4-AT-A) was purchased for evaluation. Upon completion of the testing, became the C-3.
C-3A: A modification of the standard C-3. A total of seven were delivered to the Army Air Corps (SN 29-220 through 226).
C-9: The final modification of the C-3 (actually the seven C-3As) was the conversion into the C-9 configuration.
See also C-4, C-9.

Statistics:
Crew: 2
Cruising speed: 107 mph
Ceiling: 16,500 feet
Range: 1,140 miles

Physical Characteristics:
Wingspan: 74 feet
Length: 50 feet
Height: 12 feet
Empty weight: 6,500 pounds
Gross weight: 10,130 pounds
Maximum payload: 1,725 pounds (11 passengers)

The Story
The C-3 was one of several versions of the Ford Tri-Motor (13 in all) that was acquired by the Army Air Corps in the late 1920s. The C-4 and C-9 were other versions that evolved from the famous three-engine transport.

Like other early 'C' planes, the military versions evolved from already-existing commercial versions. Such was the case with the C-3 (the first model was designated XC-3) with the basic commercial version being tested. The plane carried the company designation of 4-AT-A. Upon completion of the testing, the model received the C-3 designation.

That first C-3 used three Wright R-790-1 225 horsepower powerplants. The aircraft carried one engine on the nose, with the other two being mounted on the wings, close to the fuselage. The testing proved to be successful, and that particular aircraft was designated the C-3.

The final seven C-3 type aircraft were upgraded versions (the 4-AT-E versions) which carried higher-performance engines with the R-790-3 engines which provided an additional ten horsepower from each engine, thus slightly increasing performance for the model.

The evolution of the C-3 continued as the seven C-3As would later be converted to the C-9 configuration.

C-4 "Tin Goose"

Manufacturer: Ford-Stout
Status: Operational
Production period/total: 1929-1931/5 built

Serial numbers:
29-219
31-401 through 404

Variants:
C-4 Single aircraft (29-219) acquired in 1929 for evaluation.
C-4A Re-engined with three Pratt & Whitney 450 horsepower R-1340-11 engines. Four of this model were delivered in 1931.
C-4B Single C-4A re-engined with three Pratt & Whitney 450 horsepower R-1340-7 engines.
See also C-3, C-9.

Statistics: (C-4A)
Crew: 3
Cruising speed: 127 mph
Service ceiling: 18,050 feet
Range: 1,020 miles

Physical characteristics:
Wingspan: 77 feet, 10 inches

Length: 49 feet, 10 inches
Height: 12 feet
Empty weight: 7,500 pounds
Gross weight: 13,500 pounds
Maximum payload: 3,743 pounds (13 passengers)

The Story
The C-4 was a military version of Ford Stout Model AT-5 trimotor. The C-4 was used extensively by Admiral Richard Byrd in his 1928-1929 Antarctic explorations. On Jan 15, 1929, in a C-4 named Stars and Stripes, FC-2W2 became the first aircraft to overfly the South Pole.

The C-4 owes much of its design to a chance visit to the Ford plant by Admiral Byrd several years earlier. Byrd flew in to the plant in a Fokker F-VII, and stayed overnight as a guest of Henry Ford.

The tri-motor aircraft had just begun its first flight tests which were very disappointing. Henry Ford had ordered his engineer and designer to fix the problem. To do so, the chief engineer, John. K. Northrop, slipped into the hangar where Byrd's aircraft was parked. During the course of the night, Northrop and his assistants made molds of the Fokker's wing using copper tubes and copper sheets.

With the new template in hand, the tri-motor's wings were redesigned and performed spectacularly in flight tests. The aircraft eventually saw service around the world, thanks to a little midnight engineering.

The Tin Goose became the largest civil aircraft in the United States when it began passenger service on 2 August 1926.

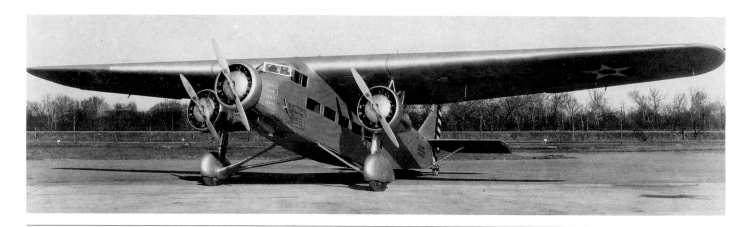

C-5 (No Nickname)

Manufacturer: Fokker
Status: Evaluation
Production period/total: 1929/1 purchased

Serial numbers:
29-405

Variants:
None, only one aircraft purchased.
See C-2, C-7.

Statistics:
Crew: 2
Cruising speed: 140 mph

Service ceiling: 18,000 ft
Range: 765 miles

Physical characteristics:
Wingspan: 79 feet, 2 inches
Length: 49 feet, 11 inches
Height: 12 feet, 9 inches
Empty weight: 7,600 pounds
Gross weight: 13,100 pounds
Maximum payload: 2,640 pounds (12 passengers)

The Story
Only one aircraft was bought for evaluation.

C-6 (No Nickname)

Manufacturer: Sikorsky
Status: Operational
Production period/total: 1929-1930/11
Serial numbers:
29-406
30-397 through 406

Variants:
C-6: Single aircraft acquired for testing at Wright Field, Ohio. After tests, it was used as a VIP transport at Bolling Field, near Washington, D.C.
C-6A: Same as C-6, but re-engined with two 450 horsepower, R-1340-7 Wright engines. Several were later adapted for target towing purposes.

Statistics:
Crew: 2

Cruising speed: 110 mph
Service ceiling: 14,200 feet
Range: 750 miles

Physical characteristics:
Wingspan: 71 feet, 6 inches
Length: 40 feet, 10 inches
Height: 14 feet
Empty weight: 7,089 pounds
Gross weight: 10,147 pounds
Maximum payload: 2,074 pounds (6 passengers)

The Story
First seaplane purchased by Army Air Corps. The C-6 was used extensively for coastal patrols in the Philippines and Panama.

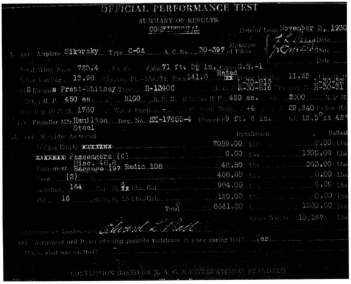

C-7 (No Nickname)

Manufacturer: Atlantic Company
Status: Operational
Production period/total: 1928-1929/11 built

Serial Numbers:
28-126 (converted C-2A), 119, 120, 123, 125 (converted C-2As)
29-407 through 412

Variants:
XC-7: Given to single C-2A converted to C-7.
C-7: The first version of this transport.
C-7A: A modified C-7 with changes in the fin and fuselage with a larger wing area.

Statistics:
Crew: 2
Cruising speed: 127 mph
Ceiling: 14,435 feet
Range: 745 miles

Physical Characteristics:
Wingspan: 71 feet, 2 inches
Length: 48 feet, 4 inches
Height: 12 feet, 5 inches
Empty weight: 6,834 pounds
Gross weight: 10,565 pounds
Maximum payload: 2,381 pounds (9 passengers)

The Story
The evolution of tri-motored transports continued in the late 1920s with the development of the C-7 from an already existing aircraft, in this particular case the earlier C-2.

In fact the initial C-7, the XC-7 prototype, was derived from a C-2A. The modification consisted of the installation of larger powerplants, the Wright R-975 engine which produced some three hundred horsepower.

Following completion of the initial testing, the XC-7 became the C-7. One of those first C-7s (28-120) established an air-to-air refueling record of 150 straight hours, the feat taking place in January 1929. The plane had the interesting name of "Question Mark."

Finally, there was the so-called C-7A which incorporated certain airframe modifications. The modifications were patterned closely after the Fokker F Xa.

C-8 (No Nickname)

Manufacturer: Fairchild Company
Status: Operational
Production period/total: 1929-1931/15 built

Serial numbers:
29-325 (XC-8 prototype)
30-388 through 30-395 (C-8)
31-463 through 31-468 (C-8A)

Variants:
XC-8: This designation was given to the single prototype. Company designation was XF-1.
C-8: The initial operation version of this model which was powered by the R-1830-7 powerplant.
C-8A: The first modification of the C-8 with an engine substitution using the R-1340-9 engine.

Statistics:
Crew: 2
Cruising speed: 108 mph
Service ceiling: 14,150 feet
Range: 625 miles

Physical characteristics:
Wingspan: 50 feet
Length: 33 feet
Height: 10 feet
Empty weight: 3,130 pounds
Gross weight: 5,000 pounds
Maximum payload: 1,240 pounds (6 passengers)

The Story

This little Fairchild creation certainly didn't look big enough to acquire a 'C' designation, but that's what it got even though its payload capability was only 1,240 pounds.

No military development program here as the C-8 was a close version of the company's already-existing Model 71 high-wing light transport which was designed for photo survey missions.

The Army Air Corps felt that the model could perform a useful military mission and tested one of the planes under the XC-8 designation.

One of the interesting characteristics of the model was the fact that it had folding wings, *a la* Navy-style aircraft. That initial prototype carried a

single fuselage-mounted R-1830-1 engine which sported a 410 horsepower capability.

The initial lot of C-8s showed a significant change in that the R-1830-7 powerplant showed an additional 40 horsepower.

Although there was no reported increase in performance with the follow-on C-8A model, there was another powerplant substitution with the R-1340-9 engine being employed.

HANDBOOK OF INSTRUCTIONS

FOR THE

C-8A CARGO AIRPLANE

(OLD DESIGNATION—F-1A PHOTOGRAPHIC)

MANUFACTURED BY

AMERICAN AIRPLANE & ENGINE CORPORATION

FARMINGDALE, LONG ISLAND, N. Y.

ON CONTRACT W535AC3780   SPECIFICATION 1682-A

NOTE: This Technical Order Replaces T. O. 01-160 dated 10-7-32.

PUBLISHED BY AUTHORITY

OF

THE CHIEF OF THE AIR CORPS

BY THE

MATERIEL DIVISION
FIELD SERVICE SECTION
WRIGHT FIELD
DAYTON, OHIO

OCTOBER 1, 1931

REVISED JULY 1, 1934. (Replaces title page revision of Oct. 31, 1933).

C-9 (No Nickname)

Manufacturer: Ford Company
Status: Operational
Production period/total: 1930/7 conversions

Serial numbers:
29-220 through 29-226

Variants:
C-9: Only designation given to model.
Note: See C-3 section.

Statistics:
Crew: 2
Cruising speed: 105 mph
Ceiling: 14,150 feet
Range: 1,100 miles

Physical characteristics:
Wingspan: 73 feet, 11 inches
Length: 50 feet
Height: 12 feet, 3 inches
Empty weight: 6,250 pounds
Gross weight: 9,985 pounds
Maximum payload: 1,700 pounds (8 passengers)

The Story

Not much of a story to tell about the C-9 transport as this particular model was a simple conversion of the C-3 into this configuration.

The change came down to the installation of more powerful engines with the substitution of the Wright R-975-1 engines which were rated at 300 horsepower each. This was a significant increase of 75 horsepower each, and the modification was made with only slight changes to the plane's airframe.

The modification was accomplished in the 1930 time period.

C-10 "Robin"

Manufacturer: Curtiss
Status: Experimental
Production period/total: 1929/1 evaluated

Serial numbers:
29-452

Variants:
XC-10: With a Warner R-420-1 engine.

Statistics:
Crew: 1 or none
Cruising speed: 84 mph
Service ceiling: 10,200 feet
Range: 480 miles

Physical characteristics:
Wingspan: 41 feet
Length: 25 feet, 8 inches
Height: 8 feet
Empty weight: 1,472 pounds
Gross weight: 2,440 pounds
Maximum payload: n/a

The Story

Only one XC-10 was purchased, and it was used for experiments in unmanned, radio-controlled flight. The "Robin" was powered by a 110 horsepower Warner Scarab engine, the R-420-1. The aircraft was scrapped in 1935 after accumulating 100 flight hours.

To perform its mission, the Robin had undergone extensive modifications, mostly involving installing the radio equipment and control system. The cowling was also significantly modified.

C-11 "Fleetster"

Manufacturer: Consolidated
Status: Operational
Production period/total: 1931/1 bought

Serial numbers:
31-380

Variants:
YC-11A

Statistics:
Crew: 2
Cruising speed: 153 mph
Service ceiling: 17,900 feet
Range: 750 miles

Physical characteristics:
Wingspan: 45 feet
Length: 31 feet, 9 inches
Height: 9 feet, 2 inches
Empty weight: 3,326 pounds
Gross weight: 5,300 pounds
Maximum payload 1,114 pounds (up to 6 passengers)

The Story
Only one Consolidated 17 Fleetster was purchased as a Y1C-11, with a 575 horsepower, Pratt & Whitney R-1860-1 engine. The aircraft was the Consolidated 17, and was used exclusively by the Assistant Secretary of War.

The aircraft was later converted to carry 17-2 standards–resulting in a passenger capacity of six–and re-engined with the Pratt R-1820-1 engine, also rated at 575 horsepower, but considered to be more reliable.

The Assistant Secretary of Defense used the aircraft in numerous fashions, mostly as official transport between Washington and various war material manufacturing sites.

C-12 "Vega"

Manufacturer: Detroit-Lockheed
Status: Evaluation
Production period/total: 1931/1 bought

Serial numbers:
31-405

Variants:
Y1C-12

Statistics:
Crew: 1
Cruising speed: 150 mph
Service ceiling: 19,750 feet
Range: 670 miles

Physical characteristics:
Wingspan: 41 feet
Length: 27 feet, 6 inches
Height: 8 feet, 2 inches
Empty weight: 2,595 pounds
Gross weight: 4,720 pounds
Maximum payload: 1,070 pounds (5 passengers)

The Story
Only one Y1C-12 Vega was acquired. Bought in 1931, it flew for four years of evaluations, gathering 999 flight hours before being scrapped.

Detroit, the manufacturer, was a predecessor company to Lockheed, and the Vega was the first aircraft Lockheed ever sold to the Army Air Corps, beginning a tradition of transport aircraft that rivals that of the Douglas Company.

It was in this John K. Northrop-designed Vega that Amelia Earhart first gained fame as the first female aviator to fly solo across the Atlantic. That flight began May 20, 1932, in Harbor Grove, Newfoundland, and ended the next day.

Vega was powered by a Pratt & Whitney Wasp engine, rated at 420 horsepower.

C-13 (No Nickname)

This will be a very short section because there was no "lucky 13" designation given to the next 'C' project. Superstition must have played a part even then.

Interestingly, when the 'C' numbering was started over again, that same number was bypassed again!

C-14 (No Nickname)

Manufacturer: American Fokker Corporation
Status: Operational
Production period/total: 1931/20 built

Serial numbers:
31-381 through 31-400

Variants:
Y1C-14: 20 were built.
C-14: The YIC after completion of tests.
Y1C-14A: A modified version of 31-400.
Y1C-14A: A modified version of 31-381.
C-14B: The Y1C-14B after completion of modifications.
Y1C-15: Conversion of 31-389, an ambulance conversion.

Statistics:
Crew: 1
Cruising speed: 133 mph
Ceiling: 14,300 feet
Range: 690 miles

Physical characteristics:
Wingspan: 59 feet
Length: 43 feet, 3 inches
Height: 12 feet, 10 inches
Empty weight: 4,530 pounds
Gross weight: 7,200 pounds
Maximum payload: 1,625 pounds (6 passengers)

The Story
In the case of the C-14, the Army Air Corps basically bought an already existing company model, the Fokker F.XIV. The aircraft is considered one of the smallest 'C' planes ever conceived.

The initial batch of 20 Y1C-14s carried a single 525 horsepower Wright R-1750 powerplant. Following completion of AAF testing, the entire fleet acquired the operational C-14 designation.

The next designation was Y1C-14A, in which a single C-14 (31-400) was re-engined with a 575 horsepower R-1820-7 engine. Later, the C-14 31-381 was re-engined, with the substitution of a 525 horsepower R-1690-5. Following completion of the latter aircraft, it acquired the C-14B designation.

Without doubt, the C-14 showed many faces during its lifetime.

C-15 (No Nickname)

Manufacturer: American Fokker Corp.
Status: Operational
Production period/total: 1931/2 conversions

Serial numbers:
31-389 plus a second aircraft

Variants:
Y1C-15: Conversion of C-14 31-389 into this ambulance configuration.
C-15A: The designation of the Y1C-15 upon completion of testing.

Statistics:
Crew: 1
Cruising Speed: 133 mph
Ceiling: 14,300 feet
Range: 690 miles

Physical characteristics:
Wingspan: 59 feet
Length: 43 feet, 3 inches
Height: 12 feet, 10 inches
Empty weight: 4,530 pounds
Gross weight: 7,200 pounds
Maximum payload: 1,630 pounds (4 litters)

The Story
Externally, the only way the C-15 varied from the C-14 was the large Red Cross painted on the fuselage of this flying ambulance.

The conversion was very minimal, to say the least, when the interior was modified to accept four stretchers.

Obviously, it was a far cry from the current C-9 Nightingale which is practically a flying hospital, but the C-15 was that first short step in that direction.

C-16 (No Nickname)

Manufacturer: General (Fokker)
Status: Evaluation
Production period/total: 1932/1 bought

Serial numbers:
32-398

Variants:
Y1C-16

Statistics:
Crew: 1
Cruising speed: 125 mph
Service ceiling: 11,000 feet
Range: 400 miles

Physical characteristics:
Wingspan: 59 feet
Length: 45 feet
Height: 13 feet
Empty weight: 4,500 pounds
Gross weight: 6,350 pounds
Maximum payload: 1,449 pounds

The Story
One Fokker Model F.XI amphibian was acquired for evaluation. Purchased as a civilian aircraft, it was registered as NC10775 (company number 1422).

This pusher aircraft was powered by one Pratt & Whitney R-1869-1 engine, rated at 575 horsepower.

C-17 "Speed Vega"

Manufacturer: Lockheed (Detroit)
Status: Evaluation
Production period/total: 1931/1 bought

Serial numbers:
31-408

Variants:
Y1C-17
See C-2, C-12, C-25, C-85, C-101.

Statistics:
Crew: 1
Cruising speed: 190 mph
Service ceiling: 26,000 feet
Range: 600 miles

Physical characteristics:
Wingspan: 41 feet
Length: 27 feet, 6 inches
Height: 8 feet, 2 inches
Empty weight: 2,595 pounds

Gross weight: 4,720 pounds
Maximum payload: 1,070 pounds (5 passengers)

The Story
When purchased, Y1C-17 was company Model DL-1b (company number 159). This aircraft was the fastest plane in the Army Air Corps in the early 1930s–cargo, fighter or bomber. The plane had a modern metal fuselage with a single-strut, wire-braced undercarriage. It also had NACA cowling for its Pratt & Whitney R-1340-17, 500 horsepower engine. Also came with wheel fairings, to reduce drag, and long range fuel tanks.

The aircraft was destroyed in an accident after only four months of service.

C-18 "Monomail"

Manufacturer: Boeing
Status: Evaluation
Production period/total: 1931/1 aircraft borrowed from Boeing

Serial numbers:
None assigned

Variants:
Y1C-18

Statistics:
Crew: 1
Cruising speed: 140 mph
Service ceiling: 14,700 feet
Range: 540 miles

Physical characteristics:
Wingspan: 59 feet, 1 inch
Length: 41 feet, 2 inches
Height: 16 feet
Empty weight: 4,626 pounds
Gross weight: 8,000 pounds
Maximum payload: 3,010 pounds

The Story
The USAAC placed an order for the Monomail, and while awaiting delivery, borrowed one from Boeing and conducted flight trials. During these tests the USAAC evidently found things not to their liking and canceled their order. Boeing continued to produce the airplanes and sold a number of them to many civilian companies.

The Monomail was powered by a single Pratt & Whitney Hornet engine, rated at 575 horsepower.

The aircraft that the USAAC borrowed had a civilian registration of NC725W, company number 1153.

C-19 "Alpha"

Manufacturer: Northrop Corporation
Status: Development
Production period/total: 1931/3 built

Serial numbers:
31-516 through 31-518

Variants:
YC-15: Carried R-1340-7 engine.
Y1C-15: Carried R-1340-11 engine.

Statistics:
Crew: 1
Cruising Speed: 155 mph
Ceiling: 19,000 feet
Range: 650 miles

Physical characteristics:
Wingspan: 43 feet, 10 inches
Length: 28 feet, 5 inches
Height: 9 feet
Empty weight: 2,800 pounds
Gross weight: 4,700 pounds
Maximum payload: 1,055 pounds (6 passengers)

The Story
This was an interesting single-engine transport in that the pilot was riding in an open cockpit, while the maximum of six passengers were in an enclosed cabin.

Only three of the tiny craft were purchased with a Pratt & Whitney R-1340 providing 450 horsepower. In an official performance test, the 31-518 Y1C-19 demonstrated a landing speed of 65 miles per hour and an absolute ceiling capability of over 20,000 feet.

The trio of Alphas (company designation Model #4) never did rid themselves of the Y limited production designation which always followed the model.

C-20 (No Nickname)

Manufacturer: Fokker
Status: Evaluated, but rejected
Production period/total: 1931/1 tested

Serial numbers:
None assigned

Variants:
YC-20: Only designation given to single plane.

Statistics:
Crew: 2
Cruising speed: 146 mph

Ceiling: 13,500 feet
Range: 740 miles

Physical Characteristics:
Wingspan: 99 feet
Length: 69 feet, 10 inches
Height: 16 feet, 6 inches
Empty weight: 14,910 pounds
Gross weight: 22,500 pounds
Maximum payload: 9,170 pounds (30 passengers)

The Story

Not much of a story to tell here, but it certainly was an interesting aircraft. The plane, company designation F-32, was a one-of-a-kind airliner. It was powered by four Hornet radial engines in tandem pairs. The plane had been used in small numbers as an airliner for Western Air Express, but due to high operating costs, it did not prove practical.

The Army Air Corps decided to evaluate the plane as the YC-20, carrying P&W R-1860-1 575 engines. The engines were interesting in that they carried propellers both on the front and rear of the engine nacelles.

C-21 "Dolphin"

Manufacturer: Douglas Corporation
Status: Operational
Production period/total: 1932/8 built

Serial numbers:
32-279 through 32-286

Variants:
Y1C-21: Initial designation of the eight models.
C-21: Designation given to models upon completion of testing period.
OA-3: Redesignated as OA-3 Observation Planes in 1933.

Statistics:
Crew: 2
Cruising Speed: 119 mph
Ceiling: 14,200 feet
Range: 491 miles

Physical characteristics:
Wingspan: 60 feet
Length: 43 feet, 6 inches
Height: 14 feet, 1 inch
Empty weight: 5,840 pounds
Gross weight: 8,561 pounds
Maximum payload: 2,721 pounds (5 passengers)

The Story
The C-21 was unique in that it was the second 'C' plane to be an amphibian, with the fuselage shaped to land softly on water. The high-mounted wing carried even higher-mounted Wright R-975 engines, each producing 350 horsepower. The C-21 was actually the military version of a Douglas commercial amphibian version.

The model saw three lives in its military career, the first designated Y1C-21 during its evaluation period. In their first operational phase, these planes carried the C-21 designation.

Finally, the decision was made that the model would serve well in a coastal defense mode. To that end, the C-21 was no longer called a 'C' plane, changing to the OA-3 observation plane designation.

C-22 "Fleetster"

Manufacturer: Consolidated
Status: Operational
Production period/total: 1931/3 procured

Serial numbers:
31-469 through 31-471

Variants:
Y1C-2.
See C-11.

Statistics:
Crew: 1

Cruising speed: 180 mph
Service ceiling: 18,000 feet
Range: 675 miles
Passenger capacity: 7

Physical characteristics:
Wingspan: 45 feet
Length: 31 feet, 9 inches
Height: 9 feet, 2 inches
Empty weight: 3,326 pounds
Gross weight: 5,600 pounds
Maximum payload: 2,157 pounds (7 passengers)

The Story

The Y1C-22 Fleetster was an improved version of the C-11, and was re-engined for better performance. The maximum payload was almost doubled to more than one ton of cargo after installation of a Wright R1820-1 radial engine. The new engine added only 300 pounds to the gross weight, but performance and payload were greatly improved.

Three of these improved Fleetsters were bought and saw operational use in the early 1930s.

C-23 "Altair"

Manufacturer: Lockheed (Detroit)
Status: Operational
Production period/total: 1932/1 procured

Serial numbers:
32-232

Variants:
Y1C-23
See C-12, C-17, C-25, C-85, C101.

Statistics:
Crew: 1
Cruising speed: 175 mph
Service ceiling: 23,800 feet
Range: 870 miles

Physical characteristics:
Wingspan: 42 feet, 9 inches
Length: 28 feet, 4 inches
Height: 9 feet, 6 inches
Empty weight: 3,235 pounds

Gross weight: 4,896 pounds
Maximum payload: 1,290 pounds (up to 2 passengers)

The Story

The Altair was bought off the shelf from Lockheed (Detroit) where it was called the Detroit Model DL-2. It was powered by a Pratt & Whitney R-1340-9, rated at 450 horsepower. The Altair was very similar to the Lockheed Y1C-25 except that it had a metal fuselage instead of the -25's wooden fuselage.

The Y1C-23 was considered by many to be the 'sporty' version of a similar model aircraft produced by Lockheed.

Like his latter day successor, General Merrill McPeak, who during his tenure as chief of staff of the Air Force had an F-15 Eagle at his disposal, the then chief of staff had the Y1C-23 for his personal use.

During flight tests in September 1931, the Altair demonstrated a top speed of 207 mph, with a stalling speed of 67 mph, and a gross weight of 4,896 pounds – stalling at only 67 mph was quite an accomplishment.

Unpressurized as all aircraft were at this time, flying above 18,000 feet was a dicey operation at best. So, although it had a service ceiling of 23,800 feet and an absolute ceiling of 25,800 feet, it is unlikely that it flew that high very often.

The plane was removed from service in 1942.

C-24 "Pilgrim"

Manufacturer: Fairchild, design from American Aircraft and Engine Corp.
Status: Operational
Production period/total: 1932/4 procured

Serial numbers:
32-287 through 290

Variants:
Y1C-24

Statistics:
Crew: 1
Cruising speed: 118 mph
Service ceiling: 13,600 feet
Range: 510 miles

Physical characteristics:
Wingspan: 57 feet, 9 inches
Length: 39 feet, 9 inches
Height: 11 feet, 6 inches
Empty weight: 4,437 pounds
Gross weight: 7,070 pounds
Maximum payload: 2,153 pounds (up to 9 passengers)

The Story
The Pilgrim was the first transport aircraft to have folding wings. This allowed more of them to be stored indoors, but did not add significantly to its utility.

Numbers vary as to exactly how many were bought by the Army Air Corps. Totals vary from four to more than twenty-five, though only four serial numbers were ever assigned to this model of aircraft.

The Pilgrim was powered by the Wright R-1820-1 engine, rated at 575 horsepower.

C-25 "Altair"

Manufacturer: Lockheed (Detroit)
Status: Evaluation
Production period/total: 1932/1 model evaluated

Serial numbers:
32-393

Variants:
None

Statistics:
Crew: 1
Cruising speed: 150 mph
Ceiling: 20,000 feet
Range: 975 miles

Physical Characteristics:
Wingspan: 42 feet, 9 inches
Length: 28 feet, 4 inches
Height: 9 feet, 6 inches
Empty weight: Unknown
Gross weight: 5,000 pounds
Maximum payload: 400 pounds (1 to 2 passengers)

The Story
Like a number of these early "C" planes, the single C-25 model was a modification of a Lockheed company model, the so-called Sirius 8A. Looking at this stubby single-engine plane, it is hard to fathom it being given the cargo designation. It looks more like a fighter/trainer-type aircraft.

The Altair was quite similar to the earlier C-23 except that the Altair still sported a dated wooden fuselage. Power was significant with a P&W R-1340-17 radial engine with 450 horsepower.

Reportedly, the Altair was the first plane to demonstrate a wheels-up landing. The plane was damaged after 153 hours of testing (presumably from that wheels-up landing) and was not repaired, thus ending the saga of the C-25.

C-26 "Dolphin"

Manufacturer: Douglas
Status: Operational
Production period/total: 1932-1933/16 built

Serial numbers:
32-396 through 32-397 and 403 through 410
33-294 through 33-297

Variants:
Y1C-26: Carried two R-985-1 powerplants. (Became the C-26).
Y1C-26A: Prototype for the C-26A.
C-26A: The Y1C-26A after tests complete.
C-26B: The C-26 with R-985-9 powerplants.
0A-4A: Modification of the C-26B.
C-29: Two C-26Bs modified to the C-29.

Statistics:
Crew: 2
Cruising speed: 117 mph
Ceiling: 12,000 feet
Range: 665 miles

Physical characteristics:
Wingspan: 60 feet
Length: 45 feet, 2 inches
Height: 14 feet, 6 inches
Empty weight: 6,257 pounds

Gross weight: 8,976 pounds
Maximum payload: 2,719 pounds (5 passengers)

The Story
The C-26 bore a marked similarity to the earlier C-21 transport carrying the same high-wing-mounted pair of R-985 powerplants. The C-26 was a civilian version of the company Dolphin 3 model; however, the company model had eight seats.

The variants were numerous, with two YIC versions (the -26 and -26A) which eventually evolved into the C-26 and C-26A models. The C-26s were converted to OA-4B observation planes, which were not used by the military but by the Treasury Department for Mexican border observation work. Two of the C-26B models then evolved as the follow-on C-29.

Through the evolution of the Dolphin, there were three types of R-985 powerplants, the -1, -5, and -9 versions.

C-27 "Airbus"

Manufacturer: Ballanca
Status: Operational
Production period/total: 1932-1933/14 built

Serial numbers:
32-399 through 402
33-18 through 27

Variants:
Y1C-27: 12-seater with cargo loading doors, eventually converted to C-27C version.
C-27A: Carried upgraded R-1860-19 engine.
C-27B: C-27A re-engined with R-1820-17 engine.
C-27C: Re-engined with R-1820-25 engine.

Statistics:
Crew: 2
Cruising Speed: 140 mph
Ceiling: 15,000 feet
Range: 500 miles

The Story
Like many of its earlier 'C' brothers, the C-27 Airbus had evolved from a montage of different models and modifications.

Initially, the military version was taken from the Company Model SP-200 civil airliner. In all, the Army bought fourteen and used the machines from 1932 through 1939. The plane was characterized by an extremely long nose with the engine mounted far forward of the cockpit.

The initial four Airbuses were bought "off the shelf" and were eventually converted to C-27C versions. The C-27A carried the 650 horse R-1860-19 engine. The C-27B showed another more powerful engine with the 675 horse R-1820-17 engine. C-27A, SN 33-19, was the model used for this conversion. The final C-27C configuration, to which thirteen of the machines would be modified, showed the final engine change with the use of the 750 horse R-1820-25 powerplant.

C-29 "Dolphin"

Manufacturer: Douglas
Status: Operational
Production period/total: 1933/2 procured

Serial numbers:
33-292 and 293

Variants:
See also C-21, C-26.

Statistics:
Crew: 2
Cruising speed: 128 mph
Service ceiling: 17,900 feet
Range: 510 miles

Physical characteristics:
Wingspan: 60 feet, 3 inches
Length: 45 feet, 2 inches

Height: 14 feet, 7 inches
Empty weight: 6,887 pounds
Gross weight: 9,616 pounds
Maximum payload: 2,729 pounds (7 passengers)

The Story

The C-29 is simply a C-26 re-engined with larger R-1340-29 Pratt & Whitney engines. The two engines were rated at 575 horsepower each.

Transport aircraft are now nearing what must have been considered a major hurdle–the 10,000 pound gross takeoff weight mark. To reach that mark, manufacturers seemed to be focusing on larger, more powerful engines, not improving airflow by reducing drag. It was the thought at the time that to get more weight in the air, more powerful engines were needed. To move that aircraft faster once it was in the air was a combination of more powerful engines and streamlining.

So as designers added larger engines, a smaller effort was made to reduce drag. As the photo indicates, there was a tremendous amount of drag inherent in the design of these early transport aircraft–the many struts used to strengthen the wings, the fixed landing gears, the nearly upright canopies, all added to the drag.

C-30 "Condor"

Manufacturer: Curtiss
Status: Operational
Production period/total: 1932/2 bought

Serial numbers:
32-320 and 32-321
Variants:
YC-30: Later designated the C-30.

Statistics:
Crew: 3
Cruising speed: 130 mph
Service ceiling: 23,000 feet
Range: 716 miles

Physical characteristics:
Wingspan: 82 feet
Length: 48 feet, 7 inches
Height: 16 feet, 4 inches
Empty weight: 12,235 pounds
Gross weight: 17,500 pounds
Maximum payload: 4,000 pounds (15 passengers)

The Story

The Condor was the last of a rapidly dying breed–the biplane. As a matter of fact, it was the last biplane purchased by the Army Air Corps. The two aircraft were used for a variety of missions, from accompanying Admiral Byrd in his Antarctic expedition in 1933 to providing V.I.P. transportation around the United States. By 1938, neither aircraft was flying; 32-321 had crashed and -320 was grounded, never to fly again in AAC stripes.

The Condor was the first cargo plane capable of carrying two tons of cargo. It was also the first cargo plane to weigh more than 10,000 pounds when empty. It was also one of the first aircraft to have retractable main gears.

When originally purchased, the rumor around Dayton (where the giant Condor underwent flight tests) was that one of the planes would be used by President Franklin D. Roosevelt and his family–the very first Air Force One!

The local paper reported that the plane was equipped with "comfortable chairs, a reclining couch and other items to provide comfort while in flight." Surely a sign that the plane was more than just a trash hauler.

Powered by two Wright 1820-23 engines, these powerful Cyclone radials produced 720 horsepower each.

C-31 (No Nickname)

Manufacturer: Fairchild (Kreider-Reisner)
Status: Experimental
Production period/total: 1934/Only 1 built

Serial numbers:
34-26

Variants:
None

Statistics:
Crew: 1
Cruising speed: 143 mph
Ceiling: 15,000 feet
Range: 770 miles

Physical characteristics:
Wingspan: 75 feet
Length: 55 feet 5 inches
Height: 15 feet 10 inches
Empty weight: 7,412 pounds
Gross weight: 12,762 pounds
Maximum payload: 3492 pounds (15 passengers)

The Story

When you look at the XC-31, you have the immediate impression that this plane was underpowered. In fact, weighing in at over six tons, this was the largest single-engine cargo plane ever built. It was also one of the most awkward-looking 'C' machines ever built.

With a 750 horsepower R-1820 powerplant, the top speed of the aircraft was only 160 miles per hour. Both the fuselage and wings were, amazingly, still fabric-covered. The craft did, however, still sport a full-retractable main landing gear.

The Army gave Fairchild the go-ahead to build the XC-31 prototype and the work was started in 1934. The first flight of the XC-31 took place in September of the same year. Even though the future was obviously pointed toward multi-engine cargo aircraft, Fairchild estimated that the single-engine configuration was more desirable from maintenance, insurance, fuel, and depreciation reasons.

The plane was tested at Wright Field under the project number of XC-941. In 1936, the C-31 lost a flyoff competition to the plane that would later be produced by the thousands, the C-47.

C-32 (No Nickname)

Manufacturer: Douglas
Status: Operational
Production period/total: 1942/25 purchased

Serial numbers:
42-53527 through 42-53532
42-57154 through 42-57156
42-57227 through 42-57228
42-58071 through 42-58073
42-61095 through 42-61096
42-65577 through 42-65579
42-68857 through 42-68859
42-70863
44-83226 through 44-83227

Variants:
XC-32: The DC-2 that was evaluated. Became the C-32 on completion of tests.
C-32A: The military version of the standard commercial DC-2 transport.

Statistics:
Crew: 3
Cruising speed: 180 mph
Ceiling: 23,600 feet
Range: 900 miles

Physical characteristics:
Wingspan: 85 feet
Length: 61 feet 6 inches
Height: 16 feet 3 inches
Empty weight: 12,295 pounds
Gross weight: 18,560 pounds
Maximum payload: 4000 pounds (14 passengers)

The Story
That oh-so-familiar profile, which would become a longtime part of military aviation, finally hit the scene with the introduction of the C-32. The model looked a lot like the famous C-47 that followed and, in fact, the C-32 was actually the first member of that famous Douglas aircraft family.

In 1942, the Army evaluated the DC-2 (they called it the XC-32) and quickly realized that they had a winner on their hands. The success caused the model to be named the C-32 after the testing was complete. The craft was powered by a pair of 750 horsepower R-1820-25 engines.

To that end, the Army bought 24 of a later version of the model, the C-32A, which had completely different powerplants–a pair of R-1820-33 engines.

The C-33 (No Nickname)

Manufacturer: Douglas
Status: Operational
Production period/total: 1936/18 purchased

Serial numbers:
36-70 through 36-87

Variants:
C-38: One of the C-33 models was later modified to the later C-38 configuration.

Statistics:
Crew: 2
Cruising Speed: 205 mph
Ceiling: 22,000 feet
Range: 1,130 miles

Physical characteristics:
Wingspan: 85 feet
Length: 61 feet, 6 inches
Height: 16 feet, 3 inches
Empty weight: 12,448 pounds
Gross weight: 18,559 pounds
Maximum payload: 2,400 pounds (14 passengers)

The Story

With the success of the C-32 passenger version, it was just a matter of time before a pure-cargo version of the same aircraft evolved. It was called the C-33.

It was improved over the C-32, though, with a strengthened cabin floor, cargo loading doors, larger tail area and a pair of R-1820-25 powerplants. It was quite a different aircraft.

It carried the company designation of Model DC.2-145, and eighteen of them were delivered by Douglas to the Army. One of those models later served as the prototype for the later C-38 transport.

The acceptance performance test of the C-33 was accomplished at Wright Field in 1936. The test aircraft demonstrated an operating speed of 171 miles per hour. The distance required to take off and clear a 50-foot obstacle was only 1540 feet. The distance required to land over the same obstacle and bring the aircraft to a stop was an impressive 1535 feet.

C-34 (No Nickname)

Manufacturer: Douglas
Status: V.I.P. Transport
Production period/total: 1936/2 bought

Serial numbers:
36-345 and 36-346

Variants:
YC-34: A VIP version of a C-32.
See also C-32, C-33, C-38, C39, C-41.

Statistics:
Crew: 4
Cruising speed: 180 mph
Service ceiling: 22,800 feet
Range: 1,060 miles

Physical characteristics:
Wingspan: 85 feet
Length: 61 feet 11 inches
Height: 16 feet, 3 inches
Empty weight: 12,325 pounds
Gross weight: 18,560 pounds
Maximum payload: 6,235 pounds (16 passengers)

The Story
The YC-34 was a variant of the C-32, only bought with a 14-seat VIP interior, used by the Secretary of War–Mr. Dern. The planes were assigned to the 1st Staff Squadron, Bolling Field, until late 1942. Cargo planes were rapidly growing bigger, and so was their cargo capacity. In less than ten years, the max payload of these workhorses had more than doubled.

These two VIP birds were powered by Wright R-1820-25 engines, rated at 750 horsepower each.

C-35 "Electra"

Manufacturer: Lockheed
Status: Experimental
Production period/total: 1936/1 purchased

Serial numbers:
36-353

Variants:
XC-35: Test version of Lockheed Electra.
See C-36, C-37.

Statistics:
Crew: 2
Cruising speed: 200 mph
Service ceiling: 31,500 feet
Range: 810 miles

Physical characteristics:
Wingspan: 55 feet

Length: 39 feet, 8 inches
Height: 10 feet, 1 inch
Empty weight: 7,940 pounds
Gross weight: 10,500 pounds
Maximum payload: 3 passengers

The Story
This test aircraft was the first Lockheed plane to carry the famed nickname of "Electra." Bought in 1936, the Electra was the first airplane with a pressurized cabin to fly above 40,000 feet (in substratosphere).

Because of it pioneering work in cabin pressurization, the planes program won the 1937 Collier Trophy, given annually to the person, program or aircraft making the most significant advance in American aviation.

After completing the high altitude tests, the XC-35 eventually landed at the Smithsonian Institute, Museum of Flight, in Washington, D.C.

The plane was powered by two experimental Pratt & Whitney engines, the XR-1340-43s, rated at 550 horsepower.

An interesting sidenote: the first Electra had a near perfect circular fuselage cross section.

C-36 "Electra"

Manufacturer: Lockheed
Status: Operational
Production period/total: 1937 through 1942/3 purchased, 26 seized from civilian use by the U.S. government

Serial numbers:
37-65 through 67, and in the 42-32000, 38000, 56000, 57000, 68000 series

Variants:
Y1C-36: Bought for evaluation, redesignated C-36 in 1937, became UC-36 in 1943.
UC-36A: Fifteen civilian planes seized by government, R-985-13, 450 horsepower engines.
UC-36B: Four seized planes, with R-1340-49, 600 horsepower engines.
UC-36C: Seven seized planes, with R-975-13, 450 horsepower engines. See also C-35, C-37.

Statistics:
Crew: 2
Cruising speed: 170 mph
Service ceiling: 20,000 feet
Range: 780 miles

Physical characteristics:
Wingspan: 55 feet
Length: 38 feet, 7 inches
Height: 10 feet, 1 inch
Empty weight: 6,426 pounds
Gross weight: 10,100 pounds
Maximum payload: 3,674 pounds (8 passengers)

The Story
The C-36 was the military designation for the Lockheed Model 10A Electra. The three aircraft purchased and the 26 seized from civilian use, mostly airliners, were modified and flew as communications platforms in the European theater of operations during World War II.

The airplane in which Amelia Earhart attempted her ill-fated around-the-world flight was a modified version of this Electra. On that flight, Earhart left New Guinea in late June in hopes of becoming the first woman to fly around the world. Her attempt ended on July 2, 1937, when her plane vanished near Howland Island in the South Pacific.

C-37 Electra

Manufacturer: Lockheed
Status: Operational, but only one procured
Production period/total: 1937/Only 1 procured

Serial Numbers:
37-376

Variants:
Y1C-37: Designation upon acquisition.
C-37: Later designation.
UC-37: Designation after January 1943.

Statistics:
Crew: 2
Cruising speed: 207 mph
Ceiling: 19,400 feet
Range: 810 miles

Physical characteristics:
Wingspan: 55 feet
Length: 38 feet, 7 inches
Height: 10 feet, 1 inch
Empty weight: 6,454 pounds
Gross weight: 10,100 pounds
Maximum payload: Unknown (8 passengers)

The Story
It's a short story on the C-37 since the Army only procured one of these twin-engine machines. The plane was identified as the Lockheed Company Model 10A. The one and only C-37 was actually built for use by the Chief of the National Guard. Following use during World War II the plane was sold, subsequently crashing in Honduras in 1947.

When the initial C-37 was procured, it carried the Y1C-37 designation. The plane was similar to the earlier Y1C-36 except for certain external detailing. The plane carried a pair of 450 horsepower R-985-13 Pratt & Whitney engines.

C-39 (No Nickname)

Manufacturer: Douglas
Status: Operational
Production status/total: 1938/35 purchased

Serial Numbers:
38-499 through 38-501
38-504 through 38-535
38-2057 through 38-2059

Variants:
C-42: Two of these C-39 models were converted into prototypes for the later C-42 model.

Statistics:
Crew: 2
Cruising speed: 155 mph
Ceiling: 20,600 feet
Range: 900 miles

Physical characteristics:
Wingspan: 85 feet
Length: 61 feet, 9 inches
Height: 16 feet, 1 inch
Empty weight: 14,287 pounds
Gross weight: 21,000 pounds
Maximum payload: 6,000 pounds (16 passengers)

The Story
The C-39 was but another of the many early variants of the famous C-47, which received a majority of the publicity for the famous-shape Douglas design.

The C-39 was a composite of military and civilian Douglas designs. The fuselage was almost identical to the DC-3 commercial airliner (also used on the C-33). It was the same case for the tail, while the Douglas B-18 bomber design donated the landing gear.

Delivery of the 35 C-39s was made to the Army Air Corps in 1939 and performed many transport duties during World War II.

Evacuation of personnel from the Philippines to Australia in the early dark days of the war was one of its most famous missions. It was also one of those C-39s that blazed the trail from Maine to Gander, Newfoundland in early 1942, the first leg of the aerial lifeline to Great Britain. One of those C-39s is presently on display at the Air Force Museum in Dayton, Ohio.

The C-39 carried a pair of Wright R-1820-55 powerplants, each capable of 975 horsepower. The plane was designed strictly for cargo-hauling duties and possessed an oversized cargo door for that purpose.

The amazing aspect of the plane, when you think of the price of military aircraft in the 1990s, was its unit cost of only $73,000 per copy! It was definitely a bargain at that price.

But its cargo mission wasn't the only job it performed. With aeronautical technology moving in giant bounds during the period, two of the C-39s served the so-common mission of a prototype. In this case, the follow-on model was the C-42, which followed shortly.

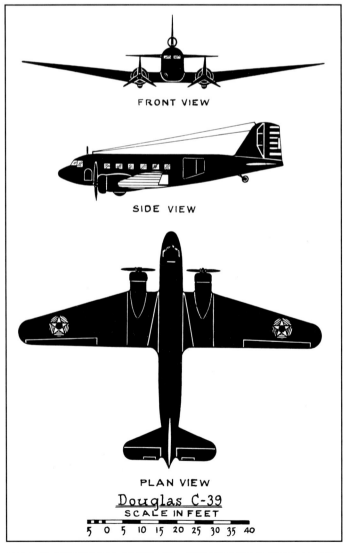

FRONT VIEW

SIDE VIEW

PLAN VIEW

Douglas C-39

SCALE IN FEET

5 0 5 10 15 20 25 30 35 40

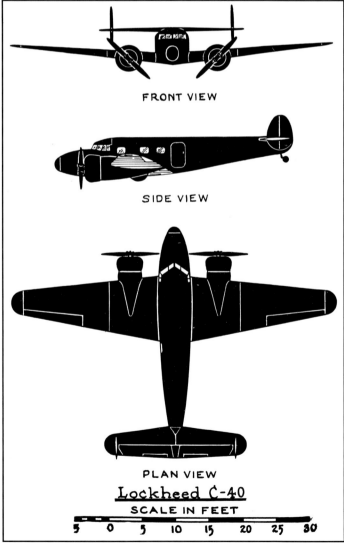

FRONT VIEW

SIDE VIEW

PLAN VIEW

Lockheed C-40

SCALE IN FEET

5 0 5 10 15 20 25 30

C-40 "Electra"

Manufacturer: Lockheed
Status: Operational
Production period/total: 1938 through 1942/24 purchased or impressed

Serial numbers:
38-536/538 (C-40)
38-539548 (C-40A)
38-582 (C-40B)
42-38280, 38346/52, 57504, 66386 (UC-40D)

Variants: (All became UC-40s in 1942.)
C-40
C-40A
C-40B
C-40C
C-40D

Statistics:
Crew: 2
Cruising speed: 206 mph
Service ceiling: 22,600 feet
Range: 824 miles

Physical characteristics:
Wingspan: 49 feet, 6 inches
Length: 36 feet, 4 inches
Height: 9 feet, 11 inches
Empty weight: 6,040 pounds
Gross weight: 8,650 pounds
Maximum payload: 2,584 pounds (6 passengers)

The Story

The C-40 (later UC-40) family were militarized versions of the Lockheed Model 12A Electra Juniors. The first fourteen aircraft were purchased in 1938 by the USAAF. The three C-40s were seven-seat passenger haulers. The C-40A had five seats, and traveled faster. The single C-40C had a fixed gear and was used as an airborne radio laboratory.

In 1942, all the designations were changed to UC-40 and an additional ten airplanes were seized from private owners and airlines. They were all designated as UC-40Ds. Five of these were later transferred to the Royal Air Force.

As a fairly light weight, twin-engined transport, the UC-40 was easily one of the faster light transports flying during the early years of the war. The Electra also was used for aerial navigation training.

All versions of this Electra were powered by twin Pratt & Whitney R-985-17 radials, cranking out 450 horsepower.

C-41 (No Nickname)

Manufacturer: Douglas
Status: VIP transport
Production period/total: 1939/2 aircraft bought

Serial numbers:
39-502, 40-70

Variants:
C-41A.
See also C-32, C-33, C-34, C-38, C-39, C-42.

Statistics:
Crew: 3
Cruising speed: 198 mph
Service ceiling: 23,500 feet
Range: 1,685 miles

Physical characteristics:
Wingspan: 85 feet
Length: 61 feet, 10 inches
Height: 14 feet, 11 inches
Empty weight: 17,525 pounds
Gross weight: 26,314 pounds
Maximum payload: 8,789 pounds (23 passengers)

The Story
The two C-41s were somewhat unusual in that the designation was given to two different modified aircraft, a C-39 and a DC-3, both with similar engines.

The C-41 was a re-engined C-39, while the C-41A was a re-engined Douglas DC-3. Both versions were powered by huge Pratt & Whitney R-1830-21 radials with 1,200 horsepower each, incredible for that time.

These large, fast, and long-legged transports were used for VIP transportation during the war. One of the aircraft was assigned to General Hap Arnold, Chief of Staff, Army Air Corps, for the duration of the war.

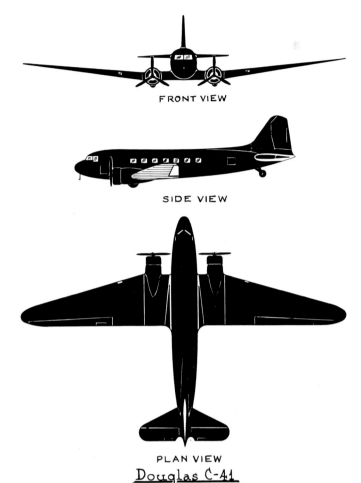

FRONT VIEW

SIDE VIEW

PLAN VIEW
Douglas C-41
SCALE IN FEET
5 0 5 10 15 20 25 30 35 40 45 50

C-42 (No Nickname)

Manufacturer: Douglas
Status: VIP transport
Production period/total: 1938/1 purchased, 2 converted from C-39

Serial numbers:
38-503

Variants:
None
See also C-32, C-33, C-34, C-38, C-39, C-41.

Statistics:
Crew: 3
Cruising speed: 170 mph
Service ceiling: 22,000 feet
Range: 800 miles

Physical characteristics:
Wingspan: 85 feet
Length: 61 feet, 9 inches
Height: 14 feet, 6 inches
Empty weight: 15,712 pounds
Gross weight: 23,624 pounds
Maximum payload: 7,912 pounds (13 passengers)

The Story
The C-42 was used exclusively as a VIP transport aircraft. Three of these VIP haulers saw service, but only one was purchased new as a C-42. Bought from Douglas Aircraft Company in 1938, it was kitted out with a VIP interior and powerful Wright R-1820-53 engines, generating 1,200 horsepower.

The two other C-42s were converted C-39s that had VIP interiors installed and their cargo doors permanently bolted shut.

The three-ship fleet was assigned to the Commander, General Headquarters, Army Air Force, and used as staff transports.

The C-42 had its last flight on May 15, 1970, piloted by Lieutenant Colonel Harold H. Sperber.

FRONT VIEW

SIDE VIEW

PLAN VIEW
Douglas C-42
SCALE IN FEET
5 0 5 10 15 20 25 30 35 40 45 50

C-43 Traveler

Manufacturer: Beechcraft
Status: Operational
Production status/total: 1939 through 1944/365 delivered

Serial Numbers:
39-139 through 39-141
42-numbers – carried designations in the 36000, 38000, 43000, 46000, 47000, 49000, 53000, 56000, 61000, 68000, 78000, 88000 94000, 97000, 107000 series
43-10818 through 43-10892
44-numbers – carried designations in the 38000, 67000, 76000 series

Variants:
YC-43: Three models were evaluated under this designation.
UC-43-BH: YC-43 with engine/equipment changes.
UC-43A-BH: Engine change to 440 horsepower R-975-11.
UC-43B-BH: Engine change to 450 horsepower R-975-17.
UC-43C-BH: Engine change to 300 horsepower R-915-1.
UC-43D-BH: Engine change to 285 horsepower R-830-1.
UC-43E-BH: Engine change to 440 horsepower R-975-11.
UC-43F-BH: Engine change to 350 horsepower R-975-3.
UC-43G-BH: Engine change to 285 horsepower R-830-1.
UC-43H-BH: Engine change to 440 horsepower R-975-11.
UC-43J-BH: Engine change to 225 horsepower R-755-1.
UC-43K-BH: Unspecified changes.
UC-43J-BH: Engine change.

Statistics:
Crew: 1
Cruising speed: 202 mph
Ceiling: 25,000 feet
Range: 670 miles

Physical characteristics:
Wingspan: 32 feet
Length: 26 feet, 10 inches
Height: 8 feet, 2 inches
Empty weight: 2,540 pounds
Gross weight: 4,200 pounds
Maximum payload: 990 pounds (4 passengers)

THE "C" PLANES

The Story

This aircraft was the Company Model 17, but it was better known as the 'Staggerwing' because of the further-forward location of the lower wing in the bi-wing configuration. Although the plane was not produced in any numbers until 1939, the aircraft type was first flown in 1932.

The plane was popular for many support missions during the war years with a significant 365 produced. Many were used by military attaches for transportation abroad. The model was also heavily used by the U.S. Navy (as the GB-1).

One of the Staggerwings is on display at the Air Force Museum.

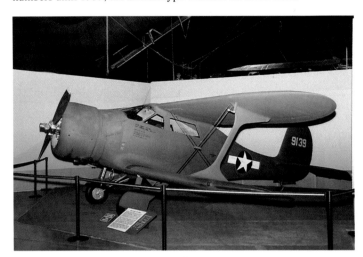

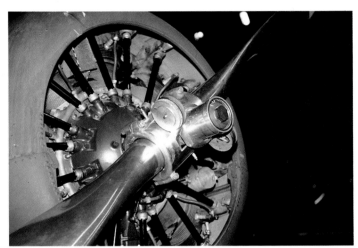

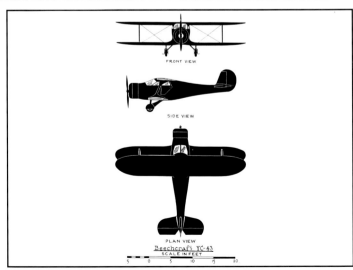

C-44 "Taifun"

Manufacturer: BFW-Messerschmitt
Status: A "loan" from Germany
Production status/total: None/1 borrowed

Serial Numbers:
39-718
Variants:
XC-44: The only designation it carried.

Statistics:
Crew: 1
Cruising speed: 161 mph
Ceiling: 19,700 feet
Range: 620 miles

Physical characteristics:
Wingspan: 34 feet, 5 inches
Length: 27 feet, 2 inches
Height: 7 feet, 6 inches
Empty weight: 1,940 pounds
Gross weight: 3,100 pounds
Maximum payload: Unknown (3 passengers)

The Story
Of all the 'C' plane stories in this book, this could be the most interesting. You see, the plane was acquired by the US Military Attaché in Berlin from German officials. This transaction took place just prior to the attack on Pearl Harbor. The plane returned to the Luftwaffe in 1940.

The single aircraft, which had a company designation of either Bf 108 or Me 108, was given the designation of XC-44, which would be the only designation it would get.

The trim little aircraft, which evolved from a 1933 design, was powered by an Argus A.S. 10cc 240 horsepower aircooled engine which cruised the machine at about 160 miles per hour.

C-45 "Expediter (Twin Beech)"

Manufacturer: Beechcraft
Status: Operational
Production status/total: 1940 through 1943/8000+ produced

Serial numbers:
Serial numbers carried 40-0000, 41-0000, 43-0000, 44-0000, 51-0000, and 52-000 series'
The model also had a number of Navy Bu. and Bul. numbers.

Variants:
C-45-BH: Used as staff transports.
C-45A-BH: Eight passenger version.
C-45B-BH: Revised interior, higher gross weight.
RC-45B-BH: Modified from F-2 reconnaissance versions.
UC-45C-BH: Engine change to two R-985-13s.
UC-45D-BH: Five-seat communications version.
UC-45E-BH: Another five-seat communications version.
UC-45F-BH: Final production model (1522 produced).
RC-45F-BH: Photo survey conversion.
C-45G-BH: Rebuilt earlier versions with navigation equipment.
TC-45G-BH: Rebuilt earlier versions.
RC-45H-BH: Photo survey version.
TC-45J-BH: Navigation training conversion.
TC-45J: Flying testbed conversion.
UC-45J: Reclassified as utility transport.
VC-45J: Classified as staff transport.
C-45T: Tricycle landing gear conversion.

Statistics:
Crew: 2
Cruising speed: 211 mph
Ceiling: 25,000 feet
Range: 900 miles

Physical characteristics:
Wingspan: 47 feet, 8 inches
Length: 34 feet, 2 inches
Height: 9 feet, 2 inches
Empty weight: 5,770 pounds
Gross weight: 9,000 pounds
Maximum payload: 1,230 pounds (6 passengers)

The Story
It goes without saying that the C-45 was one of the most prolifically produced (8000+) and most often modified of all the 'C' planes through the years. It was used for an abundance of varied missions including cargo and personnel transport, reconnaissance, navigation, research testbed, trainer, and many other missions. It was used by both the Army, Navy, and many foreign countries. The last of the C-45s was retired from USAF in 1964.

Designated as Beech Aircraft's Model 18, both the Army and Navy ordered small numbers of the craft in 1940 with the so-called Twin-Beech being produced for a record 32 years.

The Navy identified its C-45 versions as the JRB-2 (transport version), JRB-3 (reconnaissance version), and numerous others.

Through the years, the various versions of the C-45 were powered by many different powerplant versions, but most of them were rated in the 450 horsepower category.

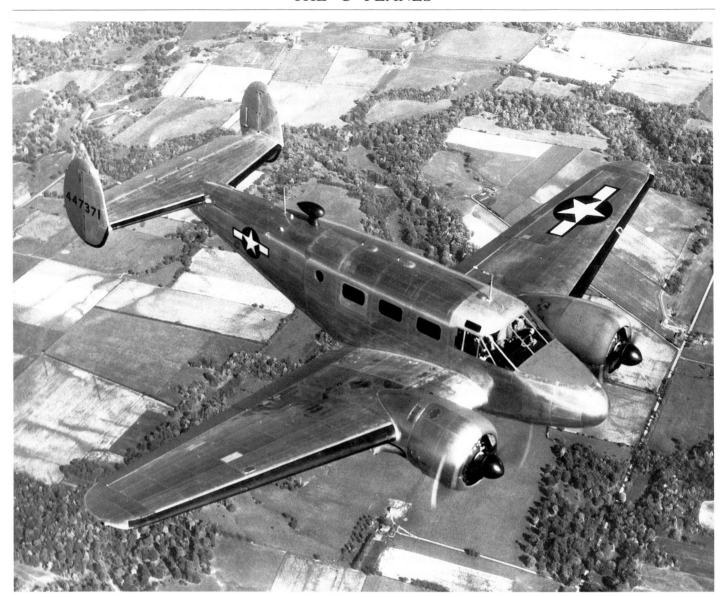

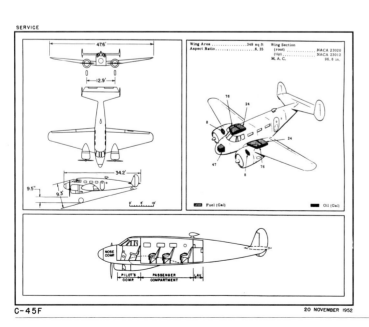

SERVICE

47.6'

12.9'

9.5"
9.3'

34.2'

Wing Area .... 349 sq ft
Aspect Ratio 6, 35

Wing Section
(root) .... NACA 23020
(tip) .... NACA 23012
M. A. C. .... 86, 6 in.

76
24
8
24
47
76
8

Fuel (Gal)
Oil (Gal)

NOSE
COMP

PILOT'S
COMP
PASSENGER
COMPARTMENT
LAV.

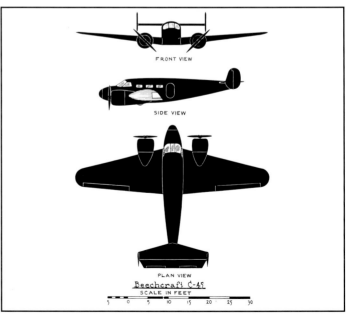

FRONT VIEW

SIDE VIEW

PLAN VIEW

Beechcraft C-45

SCALE IN FEET
5   0   5   10   15   20   25   30

C-45F

C-46 "Commando"

Manufacturer: Curtiss-Wright Corp.
Status: Operational
Production period/total: 1941 through 1944/3140 purchased

Serial numbers:
41-5159 through 5183, 5184 through 5204, 12280 through 12433, 24640 through 24775.
42-3564 through 3683, 60942 through 61091, 96529 through 96707 and many nonsequentially assigned serial numbers in the 96700 series, 96800 series, 101000 series, 101100 series 101200 series, 107200, 107300 series.
43-46955 through 47304, 47315 through 47402, 46953 through 54, 47305 through 47314, 43339 through 43340 (43341 through 43838 canceled).
44-77295 through 78544.

Variants:
C-46A: Wright R-2800-51 (2000 horsepower), single cargo doors, strengthened floor, cargo door on port side, folding seats for fifty troops.
TC-46A: At least three C-46A converted to crew trainers (42-96605, 96756, 107320).
EC-46A: Given to Japanese Air Self Defense Force. C-46A modified for airways calibration.
XC-46A: One C-46A (43-46956) temporarily used for development tests. Reverted back to C-46 status at completion of testing.
XC-46B: C-46A (43-46953) outfitted with a stepped windscreen and 2,100 horsepower R-2800-34W engines.
XC-46C: Two C-46As fitted with Rocket Assisted Take Off (RATO) gear.
C-46D: Specialized troop carrier version of C-46 with a modified door. More than 1,400 of this model Commando were purchased.
TC-46D: Fifteen C-46Ds converted to crew trainers.

C-46E: Seventeen C-46Ds modified with single cargo door, three-bladed propellers, stepped windscreen, and R-2800-75, 2000 horsepower engines.
C-46F: Same as C-46D, but powered with R-2800-75 engines. 234 bought.
C-46G: Same as C-46F, but with single cargo door and 2,100 horsepower R-2800-34 engines. Only one (44-78945) built in this configuration, eventually converted to XC-113.
C-46H: More powerful version of C-46F, with twin tail wheels. Three hundred were ordered and later canceled. One C-46A (42-107294) modified to this standard after the war.
C-46J: Designation given to a planned, but never ordered, update to C-46E.
XC-46K: Projected as a conversion of C-46F, powered by R-3350-BD, 2,500 horsepower engines.
XC-46L: Reportedly three C-46As were modified with the 2,500 horsepower, R-3350-BD engines and used as flying testbeds.
ZC-46E: Created by redesignating the C-46E in 1948.
See also C-55 and C-113.

Statistics:
Crew: 4
Cruising speed: 173 mph
Service ceiling: 24,500 feet
Range: 3,150 miles

Physical characteristics:
Wingspan: 108 feet
Length: 76 feet, 4 inches
Height: 21 feet, 9 inches
Empty weight: 30,000 pounds
Gross weight: 45,000 pounds
Maximum payload: 15,000 pounds (up to 50 passengers)

THE "C" PLANES

The Story

Like most of the transport aircraft used by the U.S. during World War II, the Commando was originally a civilian airliner converted to meet the cargo needs of a country at war. Originally designed in 1936, the Commando began operational use in 1941.

The Commando had a very distinguished career during the war, being one of the few aircraft to see service in every theater of the war.

An original order of 25 Commandos was quickly added onto when the USAAF ordered another 1,491 Commandos in the C-46A designation. This single cargo door was later supplanted by the twin cargo door C-46D. This model also had a modified nose and windscreen. Other variations of the aircraft basically differed only by which powerplant was used.

Most famous for its operations in the Far East, the Commando was a workhorse in "flying the hump," bringing desperately needed supplies to troops in China from bases in India and Burma. It flew an incredible variety of cargo, including light artillery, small vehicles, fuel, ammunition, parts of aircraft and on occasion, various types of livestock.

The Marines used the Commando in the Pacific island-hopping campaigns, flying supplies in and wounded soldiers out of numerous island landing strips.

It wasn't until March 1945 that the C-46 saw duty in the ETO–European Theater of Operations. There, it joined Ike in time to drop paratroopers in the push for the Rhine.

Though not built in the same quantities as its close cousin the C-47, the Commando nonetheless played a vital role in winning the war. Its huge cargo capacity and long range made it ideal for the vast Pacific campaign, where it played a starring role.

C-47 "Skytrain"

Manufacturer: Douglas Aircraft Company
Status: Operational
Production period/total: 1941 through 1945/10,048 purchased by USAAF, U.S. Navy, plus another estimated 2,700 built in the Soviet Union as the Lisunov Li-2. Additionally, another 1,900 flew in the twenty-five Royal Air Force squadrons as the Dakota.

Serial numbers:
41-7722 through 7866, 18337 through 18699, 19463 through 19499, 38564 through 38763.
42-5635 through 5704, 23300 through 24419, 32786 through 32935, 92024 through 93823, 100436 through 101035, 10879 through 108993.
43-15033 through 15432, 47963 through 48640, 48642 through 49032, 49034 through 49267, 49269 through 49350, 49352 through 49374, 49376 through 49702, 49704 through 49759, 49761 through 49789, 49971 through 49807, 49809 through 49813, 49815 through 49831, 49833 through 49851, 49853 through 49879, 49881 through 49902, 49904 through 49920, 49922 through 49938, 49940 through 49955, 49957 through 49962.
44-76195 through 77294, with 71 randomly placed exceptions
45-876 through 907.

Variants:
C-47: Two 1200 horsepower R-1830-92 engines, seats for 27 troops, or 10,000 pounds.
C-47A: Same as C-47, but with 24-volt electrical system.
AC-47A: Electronics calibration aircraft, later redesignated EC-47A. Designation given to gunships in 1962.
EC-47A Designation given to ex-AC-47As in 1962.
HC-47A: Designation given to ex-SC-47A, an Air-sea rescue conversion. These were later converted again, but to VC-47A, VIP transports.
JC-47A: A C-47A used temporarily for testing.
RC-47A: Converted for photographic survey purposes.
SC-47A: Originally designation for air-sea rescue conversion. See HC-47A.
VC-47A: Executive transport conversion.
WC-47A: Weather reconnaissance conversion, at least one (43-15218) flew.
C-47B: C-47A but with 1,200 R-1830-90 or 90B or -90C with high-altitude superchargers and provisions for additional fuel tanks.
TC-47B: Diverted to Navy for training purposes.
VC-47B: Converted to VIP transports.
XC-47C: One C-47 (42-5671) fitted with twin Edo Model 78 amphibious floats, each with two retractable wheels. Planned for use in Pacific. Other C-47s had the floats attached in the field.
C-47D: Basically a C-47B with superchargers removed.

AC-47D: Twenty-six converted in 1953 for electronics calibration, became EC-47D in 1962 when about twenty-five gunships, originally called FC-47Ds, were redesignated as AC-47Ds.
EC-47D: Electronic reconnaissance conversion, with R-1830-90D engines, also designation for electronic calibrations aircraft, formerly with AC-47D designation.
FC-47D: Original designation for "Puff the Magic Dragon" gunships used in Vietnam by 4th Air Commando Squadron. Fitted with three fixed 7.62 mm Miniguns on port side firing through two windows and the door, and increased fuel capacity for long loiter time. Redesignated AC-47D in 1962.
HC-47D: Redesignation of SC-47Ds.
RC-47D: Photo/electronic reconnaissance conversion of the C-47D, with two R-1830-90C or -92 engines. Turned over to South Vietnamese Air Force.
SC-47D: Rescue conversion of C-47D with a ventrally mounted lifeboat. Redesignated HC-47D in 1962.
TC-47D: TC-47Bs with superchargers removed.
VC-47D: VIP transport conversions of C-47D.
C-47E: Projected version of C-47B with two 1,200 horsepower, R-1820-80 engines. This version never flew, and designation was given to eight C-47A and Bs modernized and given R-2000-4 engines, and used by U.S. Army for airways check aircraft.
YC-47F: Super DC.3 prototype, with relocated wing, redesigned tail and other detail refinements. Evaluated by Air Force (51-3817), eventually turned over to Navy as SR4D.
C-47G: Reserved but never used.
C-47H: Designation given to Navy R4D-5s that were turned over to Air Force.
EC-47H: Designation given to Navy R4D-5Qs that were turned over to Air Force.
LC-47H: Designation given to Navy R4D-5Ls that were turned over to Air Force.
VC-47H: Designation given to Navy R4D-5Zs that were turned over to Air Force.
C-47J: Designation given to Navy R4D-6s that were turned over to Air Force.
EC-47J: Designation given to Navy R4D-6Qs that were turned over to Air Force.
LC-47J: Designation given to Navy R4D-6Ls that were turned over to Air Force.
SC-47J: Designation given to Navy R4D-6Ss that were turned over to Air Force.
TC-47J: Designation given to Navy R4D-6Rs that were turned over to Air Force.
VC-47J: Designation given to Navy R4D-6Zs that were turned over to Air Force.

TC-47K: Designation given to Navy R4D-7s that were turned over to Air Force.

C-47L: Reserved but never used.

EC-47M: Reserved for Navy Electronic Counter Measures version of C-47.

EC-47N: ECM/electronic reconnaissance version of C-47A, with R-1830-90D or 92.

EC-47P: An EC-47N, but converted from C-47D.

EC-47Q: A few C-47A and Ds re-engined with R-2000-4 engines and outfitted with classified ECM equipment.

See also C-48, C-49, C-50, C-51, C-52, C-53, C-68, C-84, C-117, C-129.

Statistics:
Crew: 3
Cruising speed: 230 mph
Service ceiling: 24,000 feet
Range: 2,000 miles

Physical characteristics:
Wingspan: 95 feet, 6 inches
Length: 63 feet, 10 inches
Height: 17 feet
Empty weight: 17,685 pounds
Gross weight: 31,000 pounds
Maximum payload: 7,500 pounds (up to 27 passengers)

The Story

One of the most famous airplanes ever built, the Skytrain, more commonly called the "Gooney Bird," saw action in three wars–something only a handful of aircraft can claim.

Used in every theater of the war, the C-47 was the backbone of the USAAF transport service. The Gooney bird flew in the heat and humidity of the Pacific to the frozen steppes of the Soviet Union. Not only did it simply carry cargo, it was the standard glider tug from 1942 onwards, playing a critical role in Operation Overlord–the invasion of France in 1944.

During the first two months of the battle for Guadalcanal, our forces there were dependent on the C-47 for all fuel, bombs and small arms ammunition, which were flown in from bases 650 miles away. On return flights, the C-47 often carried seriously injured Marines to the rear for additional medical treatment. During the Japanese invasion of Burma, one pilot reportedly crammed over 70 refugees into a Gooney Bird and flew them to safety. Another Gooney Bird towed a Waco CG4.

This versatile aircraft also was the first weather reconnaissance aircraft to fly. It was used for photo reconnaissance, electronic warfare and as the platform for the first gunship, appearing in South Vietnam in the early 1960s.

Called "Puff the Magic Dragon," the AC-47 could put a 20 mm slug in every square foot of a football field with a 3-second burst from its three electrically operated miniguns. Painted black and using red tracer rounds, the Viet Cong thought that Puff was a god, wreaking vengeance on them with its long red tongue. It soon became one of the most feared weapons in Southeast Asia, and much beloved by the "grunts".

It was on a Puff that the only enlisted Air Force Medal of Honor winner earned his award.

More than 1,000 C-47s were still on Air Force rolls in 1961, and even now thousands of Gooney Birds still ply the airways serving governments, small airlines and bush pilots around the world.

C-47B

WW II Invasion Stripes

C-47 Early research test bed

C-48 (No Nickname)

Manufacturer: Douglas
Status: Operational, commandeered DC-3As and DCT-As
Production period/total: 1941, 1942/33 commandeered from United Air Lines and 3 taken from the production line.

Serial numbers:
41-7681 (C-48) and 7682, 83 and 84 (C-48A)
42-38324 through 38326, 56089 through 56091, 56098 through 56102, 56609 through 56612, 56629 (all C-48B)
42-38258 through 38260, 38627, 38332 through 38338, 78026 through 78028, 52990 and 52991 (C-48C)

Variants:
C-48: One DC-3A intended for UAL, a 21-seater powered with two R-1830-82.
C-48A: Three impressed DC-3A, with R-1830-82 and 18-seat interiors, used for staff transports.
C-48B: Sixteen impressed DST-A, 15 from UAL, one from Northwest Airlines, with R-1830-51, 16-seat interiors, used as air ambulances.
C-48C: Sixteen impressed DC-3A, with R-1830-51 and 21-seat interiors.
See also C-47, C-49 to C-53, C68, C-84, C-117, C-129.

Statistics:
Crew: 3
Cruising speed: 192 mph
Service ceiling: 20,800 feet
Range: 1,050 miles

Physical characteristics:
Wingspan: 95 feet
Length: 64 feet, 5 inches
Height: 16 feet, 3 inches
Empty weight: 16,289 pounds
Gross weight: 24,000 pounds
Maximum payload: 3,950 pounds, (21 passengers/14 berths)

The Story
The DST-A were Pullman conversions of the DC-3, equipped with sleeping platforms that were used for overnight flights. These thirty-six impressed aircraft flew either as staff transports or as air ambulances.

C-49 (No Nickname)

Manufacturer: Douglas
Status: Operational, commandeered from airlines
Production period/total: 1940s/138 commandeered

Serial numbers:
Unknown

Variants:
Unknown
Statistics:
Crew: 3
Cruising speed: 196 mph
Service ceiling: 22,750 feet
Range: 1,050 miles

Physical characteristics:
Wingspan: 94 feet, 7 inches
Length: 64 feet, 5 inches
Height: 14 feet, 11 inches
Empty weight: 16,295 pounds
Gross weight: 24,400 pounds
Maximum payload: 3,950 pounds (up to 24 passengers)

The Story
Most were standard DC-3, but a few were the DCT (see C-48) version. All were flying with civilian airlines when the government impressed them in 1942 and 1943 for use in the war effort.

C-50 (No Nickname)

Manufacturer: Douglas
Status: Operational
Production status/total: 1941/14 were commandeered

Serial numbers:
41-7697 through 41-7700
41-7710 through 41-7711
41-7703 through 41-7705
41-7695 through 41-7696
41-7709
41-7712 through 41-7713

Variants:
C-50-DO: Ex-American Airlines planes.
C-50A-DO: Special seating for 28 troops.
C-50B-DO: Ex-Braniff Airlines planes.
C-50C-DO: Ex-PA Central Airlines plane.
C-50D-DO: Ex-PA Central Airlines plane modified for 28 troops.

Statistics:
Crew: 3
Cruising speed: 205 mph
Ceiling: 23,500 feet
Range: 1,050 miles

Physical characteristics:
Wingspan: 95 feet
Length: 64 feet, 6 inches
Height: 14 feet, 11 inches
Empty weight: 16,650 pounds
Gross weight: 29,300 pounds
Maximum payload: 3,727 pounds (28 passengers)

The Story
It was war and cargo planes were needed pronto! There were already such planes available in the domestic airline industry, and many of these were commandeered by the Army Air Corps for their critical mission. The planes came from American, Central, and Braniff Airlines.

The C-50, named by the AAC, was an early version of the venerable DC-3 airliner. Of course, it was necessary to reconfigure the planes to the military requirements. The C-50s used various versions of the Wright R-1820 powerplants, depending on the particular variant of the aircraft.

The C-51 (No Nickname)

Manufacturer: Douglas
Status: Operational

Production status/total: 1941/1 was commandeered

Serial numbers:
41-7702

Variants:
None

Statistics:
Crew: 3
Cruising Speed: 207 mph
Ceiling: 23,500 feet
Range: 1,050 miles

Physical characteristics:
Wingspan: 95 feet
Length: 64 feet 5 inches
Height: 14 feet 11 inches
Empty weight: 16,650 pounds
Gross weight: 29,500 pounds
Maximum payload: 3,730 pounds (28 passengers)

The Story
This is indeed a short story because there is only one plane to discuss with the C-5l. Like the C-50, this aircraft type (also a derivative of the DC-3) was commandeered from the airlines, in this case the Canadian Colonel Airlines.

The plane carried a starboard-side door, seating for 28 combat troops, and a pair of Wright R-1820-83 powerplants. The plane was configured for the carrying of paratroopers. Whether this plane ever carried out that mission in the heat of battle is not known from available data.

One thing that is known about the lone C-51 is that it was taken off the Army Air Corps rolls in early 1943.

C-52 (No Nickname)

Manufacturer: Douglas
Status: Operational
Production status/total: 1941-1942/5 planes commandeered

Serial numbers:
41-7701, 7706, 7708, 7714
42-6505

Variants:
C-52-DO: Ex-United Airlines version, starboard-side door, 28 seats.
C-52A-DO: Ex-Western Airlines version.
C-52B-DO: Ex-United Airlines version, detailing differences from C-52-DO.
C-52C-DO: Ex-Eastern Airlines version, port-side door and seats for 29 troops.
C-52D-DO: Ex-Swiftflite aircraft.

Statistics:
Crew: 3
Cruising speed: 196 mph
Ceiling: 23,200 feet
Range: 2,125 miles

Physical characteristics:
Wingspan: 95 feet
Length: 64 feet, 6 inches
Height: 14 feet, 11 inches
Empty weight: 18,300 pounds
Gross weight: 27,000 pounds
Maximum payload: 3,730 pounds (28/29 troops)

The Story
It's the same old story here with another variant of the venerable DC-3 (and C-47). The plane basically could have been described as similar to the C-49, only with larger powerplants.

The C-52 was used mostly for paratrooper operations. Since only five were procured, its effect on the overall war was minimal. Of greater interest was how the five planes were procured. They were actually commandeered from various airlines: United, Western, Eastern, and Swiftflite Airlines.

The standard powerplant for the C-52 was the Pratt & Whitney R-1830 which produced 850 horsepower.

C-53 "Skytrooper"

Manufacturer: Douglas
Status: Operational
Production period/total: 1941-43/404 purchased or impressed
Serial numbers:
41-20045 through 20136
42-6455 through 6504,15530 through 15569, 15870 through 15894, 47371 through 47382, 68693 through 68851
43-14404 through 405, 2018 through 2034 (2025 and 26 later diverted to U.S. Navy)

Variants:
C-53: Basically a troop transport version of C-47, with side seating for 28 troops and a port-side passenger door, and no large loading door. Powered by R-1830-92. Total of 219 of this version delivered.
C-53B: Winterized version of C-53, with extra fuel capacity and separate navigator's station. Eight built (42-20047/50, 20052, 200057/59).
C-53C: Same as C-53, but with larger port-side door. Specialized as a troop transport and glider tug. Seventeen built (43-2018-2034).
C-53D: Same as C-53C, but with 24-volt electrical system. Total of 159 built (42-68693/68851).
VC-53A: Executive transport (41-15873).
XC-53A: Single aircraft (42-6480), with full-span, slotted flaps and hot-

air leading edge de-icing equipment.

ZC-53: Designation given to surviving C-53s in 1948.

ZC-53D: Designation given to surviving C-53Ds in 1948.

See also C-47 to C-52, C-68, C-84, C-117, C-129.

Statistics:

Crew: 3

Cruising speed: 208 mph

Service ceiling: 24,100 feet

Range: 1,550 miles

Physical characteristics:

Wingspan: 95 feet

Length: 64 feet, 5 inches

Height: 14 feet, 11 inches

Empty weight: 16,295 pounds

Gross weight: 24,400 pounds

Maximum payload: 4,000 pounds (up to 42 passengers/26 paratroopers)

The Story

Called Dakota IIs, this version of the venerable DC-3 was powered by Pratt & Whitney R-1830-92, 1200 horsepower engines. The C-53 was used primarily as a troop transport and glider tug.

C-54 "Skymaster"

Manufacturer: Douglas
Status: Operational
Production period/total: 1941 through 1945/1164 for USAAF use

Serial numbers:
41-20137 through 20145, 32936 through 32950 (C-54)
41-37268 through 37319 (C-54A)
42-72165 through 72319, 107426 through 107470 (C-54A); 7230 through 7439 (C-54B); 72440 through 764 (C-54D)
43-17124 through 17198 C-54B); 17199 through 17253 (C-54D)
44-9001 through 9025 (C-54B); 9026 through 9150 (C-54E)
45-476 through 637 (C-54G), 59602 (XC-54K)

Variants:
C-54: Initial production model, four 1350 horsepower R-2000-3 engines. Accommodations for up to 50 troops. Ordered by American Airlines, the 24 aircraft were commandeered by USAAF while still on the production line. Basically an olive drab painted airliner.
C-54A: Same as C-54, but with strengthened airframe, cargo loading door, increased fuel capacity, powered by four 1290 horsepower R-2000-7 engines. 252 bought.
ZJC-54A: Single C-54A (41-37268) used for miscellaneous flight testing at Edwards AFB, California.
MC-54A: Optional designation given to C-54A when used for medical evacuation missions in 1945 and 1946.
C-54B: Same as C-54A, but with integral wing fuel tanks and provisions for carrying stretchers. 220 bought.
C-54C: Single C-54A (42-107451) converted to presidential transport, with 15-passenger VIP seating and sleeping berths for six.
C-54D: Same as C-54B, but powered by four 1350 horsepower R-2000-11 engines, total of 380 built.
AC-54D: A number of C-54D modified for use as navigation aid calibration. Redesignated EC-54D in 1962.
EC-54D: See AC-54D.
HC-54D: See SC-54D.
JC-54D: Nine C-54Ds converted for missile tracking and nose cone recovery by 6550th Operations Group in 1960 and 1961.
SC-54D: Original designation for air-sea rescue operations version of C-54D. Modified by Convair, Dallas, Texas, with additional fuel, blister windows and additional navigation and rescue equipment. Redesignated HC-54D in 1962. Official name was "Rescuemaster."
TC-54D: A few C-54Ds modified for aircrew training.
VC-54D: Staff transport conversions of C-54D.
WC-54D: Three modified for weather reconnaissance (42-72501, 72618, 72692).
C-54E: Same as C-54D, but with increased fuel capacity, convertible interior (either passenger or freight). Total of 125 built.
AC-54E: Airways calibration version, redesignated EC-54E in 1962.
EC-54E: see AC-54E.
HC-54E: see SC-54E.
SC-54E: Air-sea conversion of C-54E, at least one modified (44-9033). Redesignated HC-54E in 1962.
VC-54E: Staff transport conversion, at least two completed (44-9052, 9117).
XC-54F: Projected transport version of C-54E that was never built.
C-54G: Same as C-54E, but powered by four 1450 horsepower R-2000-9 engines–162 built in this configuration.
HC-54G: see SC-54G.
JC-54G: A few C-54Gs (including 45-506, 527, 609) used temporarily for testing.
SC-54G: Air-sea rescue version, at least two converted (45-578, 608). Redesignated HC-54G in 1962.
VC-54G: Several C-54Gs converted to staff transports (including 45-480, 484, 516, 537, 574, 624, 627, 633).
C-54H: Was to have been the designation for XC-54F, if it had been built, but powered by R-2000-9, 1450 horsepower engines.
C-54J: Same as C-54H, but with convertible interior, project only.
XC-54K: Single prototype built (45-59602), designed as a long range transport, with four 1425 horsepower, R-1820-HD engines.
C-54L: Single C-54A used for testing a modified fuel system.
C-54M: Total of 38 C-54As converted to carry coal during the 1949 Berlin Airlift.
MC-54M: Thirty C-54Es converted to medical evacuation in 1951, for use in Korean War.
VC-54M: Single MC-54M (449041) converted to executive transport.
VC-54N: Ex Navy R5D-1Z.
C-54P: Ex Navy R5D-2.
VC-54P: Ex Navy R5D-2Z.
C-54Q: Ex R5D-3.
VC-54Q: Ex Navy R5D-3Z.
C-54R: Ex Navy R5D-4R.
C-54S: Ex Navy R5D-5.
VC-54S: Ex Navy R5D-5Z.
C-54T: Ex Navy R5D-5R.
EC-54U: Ex Navy R5D-4.
RC-54V: Ex U.S. Coast Guard R5D-3P.
See also C-114, C115, C-116 and C-118.

Statistics:
Crew: 5
Cruising speed: 239 mph
Service ceiling: 22,000 feet
Range: 3,900 miles

Physical characteristics:
Wingspan: 117 feet, 6 inches
Length: 93 feet, 11 inches
Height: 27 feet, 6 inches
Empty weight: 38,000 pounds
Gross weight: 73,000 pounds
Maximum payload: 28,000 pounds (49 passengers)

THE "C" PLANES

The Story

The Skymaster was the first four-engine transport in USAAF history, as well as the largest transport built up to this time.

On June 21, 1938, the first prototype flew, with the company designation of DC-4. Intended to be the first intercontinental airliner, it did not have the legs required. Instead, this prototype was sold to Japan in 1939. Douglas designers went back to the drawing board and came up with a slightly smaller but much more efficient version, called the DC-4A.

When World War II broke out, the USAAF commandeered all 24 aircraft that were under production for American Airlines. Painted olive drab, they were essentially green airliners. However, Douglas quickly began turning out militarized versions which, like the C-47, were to have long and distinguished careers in the USAAF and later the USAF. The more than

1,000 Skymasters served the USAAF primarily as transatlantic transport for personnel and equipment. A small number were given to Great Britain under the lend-lease program and were used on ferry routes in the Far East.

The "Sacred Cow," a C-54C, became the first presidential aircraft and was used extensively by President Roosevelt during the war years, and by President Truman later. Also, a C-54B (43-17126) was transferred to the Royal Air Force and was assigned to No. 246 Squadron as Prime Minister Churchill's personal aircraft.

During Operation Vittles, commonly known as the Berlin Airlift, nearly every C-54 in the inventory flew around-the-clock missions carrying food, coal, flour and other essential goods (including candy for the children) into the besieged city.

XC-55 (No Nickname)

Manufacturer: Curtiss
Status: Experimentation
Production period/total: 1941/1 produced for testing

Serial numbers:
41-21041

Variants:
None
See also C-46, C-113.

Statistics:
Crew: 4
Cruising speed: 222 mph
Service ceiling: 26,900 feet
Range: 1,500 miles

Physical characteristics:
Wingspan: 108 feet, 1 inch
Length: 76 feet, 4 inches
Height: 21 feet, 9 inches
Empty weight: 27,600 pounds
Gross weight: 40,000 pounds
Maximum payload: unknown (36 passengers)

The Story
One company model CW-20 was purchased in 1941 and was developed into the C-46 Commando. The main difference being that the company model had a twin tail which was changed to a single fin during testing.

This aircraft was impressed in October 1941 and eventually was given to Britain and entered British Overseas Airline Company as a commercial airliner called "Spirit of St. Louis." It was broken up in 1943.

The XC-55 was powered by two Wright R-2600 engines with 1,700 horsepower each.

C-57 "Lodestar"

Manufacturer: Lockheed
Status: Operational
Production status/total: 1941-1943/20 were commandeered

Serial numbers:
41-19730 through 19732, 23164 through 23170
43-34921 through 34923, 3271 through 3277

Variants:
C-57-LO: Powered by two 1200 horsepower R-1830-53 Pratt & Whitney engines.
C-57A-LO: Special designation.
C-57B-LO: Specially equipped for troops.
C-57D-LO: Powered by two R-1830-92 engines.

Statistics:
Crew: 4
Cruising speed: 260 mph
Ceiling: 23,400 feet
Range: 2,000 miles

Physical characteristics:
Wingspan: 65 feet, 6 inches
Length: 49 feet, 10 inches
Height: 11 feet, 10 inches
Empty weight: 11,630 pounds
Gross weight: 20,500 pounds
Maximum payload: 2,160 pounds (18 passengers)

The Story

If you thought the C-57 looked a lot like the earlier C-56, you would be correct. The lone difference between the pair of Lockheed aircraft was the later version's R-1830 powerplant.

Like a number of World War II-vintage aircraft, the twenty C-57 Lodestars were all commandeered for wartime use. There were four variants of the basic model, most of the changes coming from the use of different powerplants.

C-58 "Bolo"

Manufacturer: Douglas
Status: Research
Production status/total: 1941/2 conversions

Serial numbers:
Not available

Variants:
C-58-DO: Only designation for C-58.

Statistics:
Crew: 3
Cruising speed: 170 mph
Ceiling: 23,500 feet
Range: 1,020 miles

Physical characteristics:
Wingspan: 90 feet
Length: 57 feet, 10 inches
Height: 15 feet, 2 inches
Empty weight: 16,320 pounds
Gross weight: 24,000 pounds
Maximum payload: 7,680 pounds (12 passengers)

The Story

The C-58 was one of the most interesting 'C' planes, having been initially developed as a bomber, the B-18.

It was assessed that the B-18 would make a good transport aircraft, so a program was initiated using a pair of B-18As which were stripped of all armament along with other modifications. The Wright R-1820 powerplants were retained for the new mission.

In a similar conversion, several other later-version B-18s, A and B variants, were given the same change of mission. These planes, though, for some reason never received the 'C' designation even though they certainly deserved it.

C-59 "Lodestar"

Manufacturer: Lockheed
Status: Operational, by RAF
Production period/total: 1941/10 bought

Serial numbers:
41-29623 through 29632

Variants:
None
See also C-56, C-57, C-60, C-66, C-111.

Statistics:
Crew: 2
Cruising speed: 236 mph
Service ceiling: 20,400 feet
Range: 1,800 miles

Physical characteristics:
Wingspan: 65 feet, 6 inches
Length: 49 feet, 9 inches
Height: 11 feet, 10 inches
Empty weight: 11,290 pounds
Gross weight: 17,500 pounds
Maximum payload: 6,210 pounds (16 passengers)

The Story

The USAAC bought ten of the Lockheed Model 18-07 Lodestars, powered by Pratt & Whitney R-1680-25, 875 horsepower engines, and turned them all over to the Royal Air Force under the Lend-Lease Act. The C-59 is similar to the C-57 (also called Lodestar) but flew with more powerful engines.

C-60 "Lodestar"

Manufacturer: Lockheed
Status: Operational
Production period/total: 1941 through 1943/361 bought, about 50 diverted to RAF

Serial numbers:
41-29633 through 2947 (C-60)
42-32166 through 80, 108787 through 92 (C-60); 32181 through 232, 55845 through 56084 (C-60A)
43-16433 through 66 (C-60A)

Variants:
C-60: Powered by two 1,200 horsepower, Wright R-1820-87 engines, seats for 14 troops, 36 delivered.
C-60A: Same as C-60, but equipped for paratroop operations, with accommodations for 18 paratroopers, 325 built.
XC-60B: One C-60A (42 - 55860) fitted with experimental de-icers that blew hot air on the wing leading edge.
See also C-56, C-57, C-59, C-111.

Statistics:
Crew: 3
Cruising speed: 270 mph
Service ceiling: 30,000 feet
Range: 1,450 miles

Physical characteristics:
Wingspan: 65 feet, 8 inches
Length: 49 feet, 10 inches
Height: 12 feet, 10 inches
Empty weight: 12,000 pounds
Gross weight: 21,000 pounds
Maximum payload: approximately 5,000 pounds (up to 18 passengers)

The Story
Finally, the last Lockheed aircraft to be called the "Lodestar"–the C-60 was an improved version of the C-56, 57 and 59.

Among the least functional of the commercial aircraft bought by the USAAF during the war, the C-60 was used for training and personnel transport. They were modified for use as paratroop platforms, although very few were actually assigned to the Troop Carrier Command. Also flown as gunner trainers, navigator trainers, and as a tug for the advanced glider school during its career in the USAAF.

Though it did not excel as a hauler, the C-60 was in demand as staff transport due to its long range and relatively large payload capability.

Many of the planes were diverted to RAF use as they came off the production line, where they flew as the "Lodestar."

C-61 "Forwarder"

Manufacturer: Fairchild
Status: Operational
Production period/total: 1941 through 1944/992 built (831 to RAF)

Serial numbers:
41-38764 through 863 (UC-61)
42-13572 through 13583, 32117 through 32165, 94147, 97053 (UC-61);
53523 (UC-61B); 70862 (UC-61C); 78031, 78033, 88619 (UC-61D); 78041,
88637, 94139 (UC-61E); 88613, 97419 (UC-61F); 94127, 97433 (UC-61G);
97414 (UC-61H); 107276 (UC-61L)
43-14408 through 14916 (UC-61A); 14917 through 15032 (UC-61K)
44-83036 through 83225 (UC-61K)

Variants: Originally called the UC-86, redesignated UC-61 when production began.
UC-61: Military version, Fairchild Model F24, 165 horsepower, Warner R-500-1 engine. All 161 of this version were delivered to RAF under Lend-Lease Act.
UC-61A: Same as UC-61, but with a radio and 24-volt electrical system. Of the 509 built, 364 went to RAF.
UC-61B: Single impressed Model 24J, with 145 horsepower Warner Super Scarab radial.
UC-61C: Single F24A-9 impressed by USAAF.
UC-61D: Three impressed Model 51As.
UC-61E: Three impressed Model 24K, with 165 horsepower Ranger 6-410-B engine.
UC-61F: Two impressed Model 24R-9.

UC-61G: Two impressed Model 24W-40.
UC-61H: Single impressed Model 24H, powered by 150 horsepower, Ranger 6-390-D3.
UC-61J: One impressed Model 24-C8F two-seater with 150 horsepower, Ranger 6-390-D3.
UC-61K: With 200 horsepower, L-440-7, 306 built for delivery to RAF.
ZC-61K: All surviving UC-61 were redesignated in 1948 awaiting disposal.
See also C-86.

Statistics:
Crew: 1
Cruising speed: 125 mph
Service ceiling: 12,600 feet
Range: 463 miles

Physical characteristics:
Wingspan: 36 feet, 4 inches
Length: 25 feet, 10 inches
Height: 7 feet, 7 inches
Empty weight: 1,813 pounds
Gross weight: 2,882 pounds
Maximum payload: 516 pounds (3 passengers)

The Story
Not much of a USAAF story here. More than 80 percent of the Forwarders were delivered to the RAF for their use. In the RAF, the UC-61 was called the Argus.

C-62 (No Nickname)

Manufacturer: Waco
Status: Mock-up
Production status/total: 1942/None produced

Serial numbers:
Projected numbers: 42-12554 through 12566, 35584 through 35823

Variants:
YC-62: Only one model under construction.

Statistics (Projected):
Crew: 2
Cruising speed: 150 mph
Ceiling: 17,000 feet
Range: 600 miles

Physical characteristics:
Wingspan: 100 feet
Length: 73 feet, 10 inches
Height: 19 feet, 1 inch
Empty weight: 21,660 pounds
Gross weight: 29,500 pounds
Maximum payload: 4,500 pounds (22 passengers)

The Story
"What might have been" is the best way to describe the canceled YC-62 program. The Waco transport creation, which was fabricated largely of wood, had a projected production of over 260 aircraft, but it was not to be.

Well-known for its construction of gliders, the Waco Company gave the YC-62 the same look. The model featured a high wing with a pair of 1,200 horsepower R-1830-92 powerplants. The design was revolutionary for the time period, with a bulbous forward fuselage and a twin tail. The outer skin of the wing and fuselage was of mahogany plywood, bonded directly to the stringers.

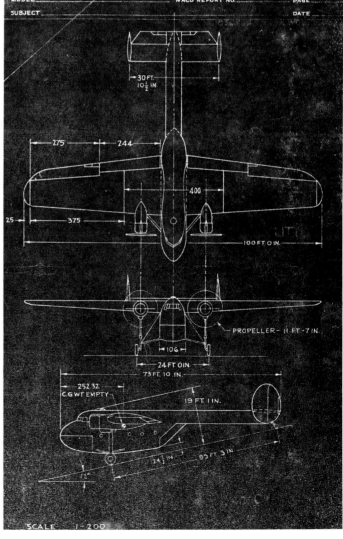

C-63 "Hudson III"

Manufacturer: Lockheed
Status: Program canceled
Production status/total: 1942/None produced

Serial numbers:
None

Variants:
None

Statistics (Projected):
Crew: 2
Cruising speed: 205 mph
Ceiling: 26,500 feet
Range: 1,500 miles

Physical characteristics:
Wingspan: 65 feet, 6 inches
Length: 44 feet, 3 inches
Height: 11 feet, 11 inches
Empty weight: 12,800 pounds
Gross weight: 18,500 pounds
Maximum payload: 1,600 pounds (17 passengers)

The Story
Like a number of other programs during the World War II era, the C-63 was one of the fatalities of the quickly-moving aircraft development scene.

The plane was to be a twin-engine low-wing transport carrying a pair of Wright R-1820 powerplants, 1,200 horsepower each. The projected 'C' plane was identified as Company Model #414. It was provisionally known as the C-63-LO.

The C-63 would have been very similar to the A-29A and C-111 models.

C-64 "Norseman"

Manufacturer: Noorduyn
Status: Operational
Production status/total: 1942-1945/759 purchased

Serial numbers:
42-5044 through 5049, 13602
43-5109 through 43-7208, 35326 through 35445
44-70255 through 70554
45-41736 through 41764

Variants:
YC-64-ND: Norseman IVs purchased for testing
UC-64A ND: USAAF version of the Norseman (initially called the C-64A-ND)
UC-64B-ND: Fitted with floats

Statistics:
Crew: 1
Cruising speed: 134 mph
Ceiling: 14,000 feet
Range: 442 miles

Physical characteristics:
Wingspan: 51 feet, 6 inches
Length: 34 feet, 3 inches
Height: 10 feet, 1 inch
Empty weight: 5,020 pounds
Gross weight: 7,540 pounds
Maximum payload: 1,690 pounds (8 passengers)

The Story
One of the most used, highest-production 'C' planes that was used during World War II, the Canadian-built U-64 served well on both land and water. It was a versatile machine (staying on operational duty until the early 1950s) and served as an air ambulance and as a navigation trainer.

The single-engined, high-wing transport was powered by several different powerplants including versions of the R-1340 and R-1340 engines.

The Army Corps of Engineers was the main user of the Norseman in its float configuration. The model was also heavily used by the Royal Canadian Air Force.

The C-64 sported a welded chrome mold steel tube fuselage structure with stubs for wing attachment. The fuselage was covered with aluminum panes at the front end and fabric aft of the cockpit. The doors were of metal and wood construction and could be completely removed to form a large freight load opening.

Of interest was the fact that the high wing was externally braced and fabric-covered. Even though the plane was entering a new era of aeronautical technology, the old methods were still in place for the model which carried the Company Model designation of Mark VI.

C-65 "Skycar"

Manufacturer: Stout
Status: Evaluation
Production period/total: 1942/1 procured

Serial numbers:
42-7772

Variants:
XC-65: original designation.

Statistics:
Crew: 1
Cruising speed: 110 mph
Service ceiling: unknown
Range: unknown

Physical characteristics:
Wingspan: 35 feet
Length: 20 feet, 5 inches
Height: unknown
Empty weight: unknown
Gross weight: 1,550 pounds
Maximum payload: unknown (1 passenger)

The Story
One of the most unusual designs tested by the USAAF, the Skycar was a commercial aircraft bought for evaluation. Evidently it did not make a big impression, as it was never bought. Because it was slow and underpowered, it did not carry much of a cargo and was never really in the running for a contract. The Skycar was the first "pusher" aircraft – with the engine facing the rear, "pushing" the plane forward – evaluated by the military.

C-66 "Lodestar"

Manufacturer: Lockheed
Status: Operational, by Brazilian Air Force
Production period/total: 1942/1 commandeered

Serial numbers:
42-13567

Variants:
None
See also C-56, C-56, C-59, C-60, C-111.

Statistics:
Crew: 2
Cruising speed: 269 mph (max)

Service ceiling: 23,400 feet
Range: 2,000 miles

Physical characteristics:
Wingspan: 65 feet, 6 inches
Length: 49 feet, 10 inches
Height: 12 feet, 10 inches
Empty weight: 11,632 pounds
Gross weight: 17,500 pounds
Maximum payload: 2,164 pounds (11 passengers)

The Story
This twin-tail version of the Lodestar was commandeered off the production line and given to the Brazilian Air Force, which used it as their "Air Force One" for then-President Getulio Vargas.

C-67 "Dragon"

Manufacturer: Douglas
Status: Operational
Production period/total: Built as B-23 in 1939, converted in 1943/12 converted

Serial numbers:
39-35, 38, 41, 47, 53 (others unobtainable)

Variants:
UC-67: converted B-23 bomber, powered by two 1,600 horsepower Wright R-2600 engines.
See also C-58.

Statistics:
Crew: 3
Cruising speed: 225 mph
Service ceiling: 26,000 feet
Range: 1,200 miles

Physical characteristics:
Wingspan: 92 feet
Length: 58 feet, 4 inches
Height: 18 feet, 6 inches
Empty weight: 19, 329 pounds
Gross weight: 26,500 pounds
Maximum payload: 7,171 pounds (21 passengers)

The Story
Beginning life as the B-23 bomber, the C-67 (redesignated UC-67 in 1943) was born when twelve were converted to utility transports with provisions for towing gliders.

The serial numbers for the C-67 are incomplete and there are some records that indicate that as many as twenty-four B-23s were actually converted.

C-68 (No Nickname)

Manufacturer: Douglas
Status: Limited operational use
Production status/total: 1942/2 commandeered

Serial numbers:
42-14297 and 14298

Variants:
None

Statistics:
Crew: 3
Cruising speed: 230 mph
Ceiling: 23,200 feet
Range: 2,125 miles

Physical characteristics:
Wingspan: 95 feet
Length: 64 feet, 5 inches
Height: 14 feet, 11 inches
Empty weight: 16,900 pounds
Gross weight: 26,700 pounds
Maximum payload: 9,000 pounds (21 passengers)

The Story

The two-plane fleet of C-68s (actually C-68-DOs) was typical of the aircraft of the period; the two planes were commandeered for military use.

The planes were actually DC-3A-414s which were equipped with a pair of 1200 horsepower R-1820-92 radials with the capability of transporting 21 troops. Interestingly, the first of the two aircraft were transferred to the Royal Air Force (RAF) for its use.

C-69 "Constellation"

Manufacturer: Lockheed
Status: Operational
Production status/total: 1942 through 1943/22 produced

Serial numbers:
42-94549 through 94561
43-10309 through 43-10317

Variants:
C-69-LO: Original commercial version which had been ordered by TWA and PanAm.
C-69A-LO: Designation given to a planned 100 troop version. Never developed.
C-69B-LO: A version planned for 94 troops.
C-69C-LO: Designation for VIP version of the C-69.
C-69D-LO: Projected version carrying 57 troops.
XC-69E-LO: Re-engined with four 2000 horsepower R-2800 engines.

Statistics:
Crew: 7 to 9
Cruising speed: 275 mph
Ceiling: 25,000 feet
Range: 3,400 miles

Physical characteristics:
Wingspan: 123 feet
Length: 95 feet, 1 inch
Height: 18 feet, 8 inches
Empty weight: 55,350 pounds
Gross weight: 86,500 pounds
Maximum payload: 15,250 pounds (60 passengers)

The Story

The war was heating up and the need for transport aircraft was huge. Therefore, 22 Constellations were diverted from airline use into military service. The model was carried with a company designation of #L049 which first took to the air in 1943. Interestingly, this model was designed by the legendary Howard Hughes. After their military use, nineteen of these were sold to the airlines. As can be seen above, there were a number of different variants of the model planned, but a number of them were never completed.

C-70 "Nightingale"

Manufacturer: Howard
Status: Operational
Production status:/total: 1936 through 1939/20 commandeered

Serial numbers:
42-38264, 38364 through 38366, 43618, 43627, 47390, 47451, 49075, 49076, 53004, 53010, 53533, 63351, 68338, 68674, 88615, 88616, and 107279.
44-32667.

Variants:
UC-70-HO: Model DCA.15P, powered by an R-985-33 450 horsepower engine.
UC-70A-HO: Powered by R-915-1 300 horsepower engine.
UC-70B-HO: Revised A variant.
UC-70C-HO: Powered by 350 horsepower R-760-1 engine.
UC-70D-HO: Powered by 285 horsepower R-830-1 engine.

Statistics:
Crew: 1
Cruising speed: 191 mph
Ceiling: 21,500 feet
Range: 955 miles

Physical characteristics:
Wingspan: 38 feet
Length: 24 feet, 10 inches
Height: 8 feet, 5 inches
Empty weight: 2,700 pounds
Gross weight: 4,400 pounds
Maximum payload: 700 pounds (4 passengers)

The Story
This single-engined 'C' plane acquired its military status like many others: the twenty that made it were commandeered. Although they were built from 1936 through 1939, they acquired 42- and 44-serial numbers.

The mission of this small high-wing aircraft was a samaritan mission as the planes were converted into flying ambulances. The appropriate 'Nightingale' name would be used many decades later with a modified DC-9 (and called the C-9) performing the same humanitarian mission.

C-71 "Executive"

Manufacturer: Spartan
Status: Operational
Production period/total: 1942/16 impressed

Serial numbers:
42-38265 through 38269, 38286 through 38288, 38367 through 38369, 43846, 57514 and 57515, 68361, 78037

Variants:
UC-71: staff transport, with 400 horsepower Pratt & Whitney Wasp R-985-33 engines.

Statistics:
Crew: 1
Cruising speed: 200 mph

Service ceiling: 24,000 feet
Range: 900 miles

Physical characteristics:
Wingspan: 39 feet
Length: 26 feet, 10 inches
Height: 8 feet
Empty weight: 2,987 pounds
Gross weight: 4,400 pounds
Maximum payload: 783 pounds (up to 4 passengers)

The Story
Sixteen Model 7W Executive five-seat single-engined monoplanes were commandeered off the production line for use as staff transports.

C-72 (No Nickname)

Manufacturer: Waco
Status: Operational
Production period/total: 1942/44 commandeered

Serial numbers:
42-38271 through 38273, 382370 and 38271, 43648, 46912 and 46913, 47391, 53512, 78036 and 94132 (UC-72); 68676 (UC-72A); 68678, 94144, 94145 and 97043 (UC-72B); 68341 and 68342 (UC-72C); 78016 and 78038 (UC-72D); 78035, 88633, 94146 and 97423 (UC-72E);88614 (UC-72F); 88621 (UC-72G); 94129, 94131, 94138, 97052 and 97416 (UC-72H); 88635, 97418 and 97425 (UC-72J); 94126 and 94141 (UC-72K); 94125 (UC-72L); 94135 and 97429 (UC-72M); 94143 (UC-72N); 97041 and 97422 (UC-72P); 97421 (UC-72Q)

Variants:
UC-72: Twelve impressed Model SRE five-seaters, powered by 400 horsepower Pratt & Whitney R-985-33.
UC-72A: One Model ARE five-seater powered by Pratt's 300 horsepower R-915-1.

UC-72B: Four Model EGD8 five-seaters with 350 horsepower R-760-E2.
UC-72C: Two impressed Model HRE five-seaters with 300 horsepower, R-680-9.
UC-72D: Two Model VKS7 five-seaters, with 240 horsepower R-830-1.
UC-72E: Two Model ZGC7 five-seaters, with 285 horsepower, R-830-1.
UC-72F: Single Model CUC1 four-seater powered by 250 horsepower R-760E.
UC-72G: Single Model AQC6 four-seater, with 300 horsepower R-915-1.
UC-72H: Five impressed Model ZQC6 five-seaters, with 285 horsepower R-830-1.
UC-72J: Three Model AVN8 five-seaters, with 300 horsepower R-915-1.
UC-72K: Two Model YKS7 four-seaters, with a 225 horsepower R-755-1.
UC-72L: Single Model ZVN8 five-seater, with a 300 horsepower R-915-1.
UC-72M: Two Model ZKS7 four-seaters, with a 285 horsepower R-830-1.
UC-72N: Single Model YOC1 four-seater, with a 285 horsepower R-830-1.
UC-72P: Two Model AGC8 four-seaters, with a 300 horsepower R-915-1.
UC-72Q: Single Model ZQC five-seater, with a 285 horsepower R-830-1.

Statistics:
Crew: 1
Cruising speed: 170 mph
Service ceiling: 23,500 feet
Range: 1,070 miles

Physical characteristics:
Wingspan: 34 feet, 9 inches
Length: 27 feet, 10 inches
Height: 8 feet, 8 inches
Empty weight: 2,734 pounds
Gross weight: 4,200 pounds
, Maximum payload: 499 pounds (up to 4 passengers)

The Story
Originally built from 1936 to 1939, these 44 Waco aircraft were commandeered from their owners for the war effort.

It must have been a big pain in the neck to group so many different models of an airplane into one designation. Of the 44 Waco commandeered, no more that twelve were of the same model. Altogether, fifteen different models of the Waco biplane are lumped into the UC-72 category. The many designations reflect the many different combinations of powerplant, airframe design, and series of design that were used by Waco. On the company models with a number as the fourth digit, that number indicates which year it was produced, 1936 to 1938.

C-73 (No Nickname)

Manufacturer: Boeing
Status: Operational
Production status/total: 1942/27 Commandeered (38 saw military service)

Serial numbers:
42-38274 and 42-30275, 56642, 57153, 57208 through 57211, 57508 through 57509, 61094, 68336, 68363 through 68373,68853 through 68854, 68859, and 78017

Variants:
C-73-BO: The only C-73 designation.

Statistics:
Crew: 2
Cruising speed: 189 mph
Ceiling: 25,400 feet
Range: 745 miles

Physical characteristics:
Wingspan: 74 feet
Length: 51 feet, 7 inches
Height: 12 feet, 2 inches
Empty weight: 9,140 pounds
Gross weight: 13,650 pounds
Maximum payload: Not Available (10 troops)

The Story
The C-73 was probably more famous in its civilian capacity where it was the plane that lost out to the DC-2 airliner in a head-to-head competition. In military garb, the C-73 (far from the sleekest transport aircraft ever constructed) had 38 of its number appear in military markings, 27 of which were commandeered from the airlines.

For the C-73 application, the existing engines were replaced with Pratt & Whitney R-1340-53 powerplants. At the end of the war, 19 of the C-73s went back to commercial service.

The C-73 also saw considerable foreign service, with the Royal Canadian Air Force taking delivery of eight of the aircraft. One of the Canadian C-73s eventually ended up with the British Royal Air Force. There also was a pair of the 247 commercial versions that served in China at the beginning of the war.

The main mission performed by the C-73 was the ferrying of aircrews into position. None of the C-73s made it until the end of the war, all being sold in 1944.

The model did have some significant firsts, though, as it was the first low-wing, all-metal, twin-engine production aircraft. Other technology advancements the C-73 displayed were rubber de-icing boots and variable pitch propellers.

C-74 "Globemaster"

Manufacturer: Douglas
Status: Operational
Production period/total: 1942/14 delivered, 36 canceled

Serial numbers:
42-65402 through 65415

Variants:
C-74: Powered by Pratt & Whitney 3,000 horsepower R-4360-27 or 3,500 horsepower R-4360-49 engines.
See also C-124.

Statistics:
Crew: 5 plus relief crew of 4
Cruising speed: 260 mph
Service ceiling: 30,000 feet
Range: 7,200 miles

Physical characteristics:
Wingspan: 173 feet, 3 inches
Length: 124 feet, 2 inches
Height: 43 feet, 9 inches
Empty weight: 86,172 pounds
Gross weight: 165,000 pounds
Maximum payload: 72,160 pounds with minimum fuel load; otherwise 50,000 pounds (125 troops/115 litters)

The Story
Only fourteen of these behemoths were delivered to the USAAF while another thirty-six on order were canceled. Though these Globemasters were all given 1942 serial numbers, the first flight did not occur until 1945 and the fourteenth aircraft was delivered in 1947.

THE "C" PLANES

The Globemaster I had several features that made it a unique airlifter. Most obvious is the "bug eye" cockpits, which seated the pilot and copilot in separate cockpits. The unusual look gave each pilot a 360 degree view of the exterior, so it wasn't all for naught; but it was impractical in two ways. One, it physically separated the two pilots, which reduced their efficiency as a team, and two, it created high drag, affecting fuel consumption (which translates to reduced range).

Another unusual aspect was its self-contained loading elevator. Able to lift up to 30 tons, the elevator made quick work of loading and minimized the need for ground equipment.

Each giant Pratt engine turned a three-bladed prop that was nearly 17 feet in diameter. Despite the huge size and heavy weight, the C-74 had a stalling speed of less than 100 knots.

The last of the Globemaster was retired in 1955. Aircraft 42-65406 was converted to YC-124, the Globemaster II prototype.

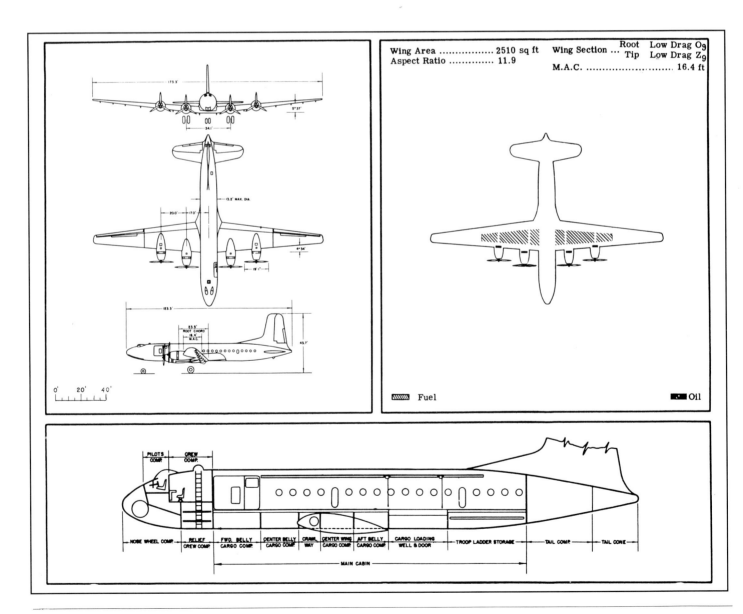

Wing Area .... 2510 sq ft	Wing Section ... Root	Low Drag O$_9$
Aspect Ratio 11.9	Tip	Low Drag Z$_9$
	M.A.C. .... 16.4 ft	

Fuel

Oil

Standard Aircraft Characteristics

BY AUTHORITY OF
COMMANDING GENERAL
AIR MATERIEL COMMAND
U.S. AIR FORCE

FOUR R-4360-49

PRATT-WHITNEY

C-75 'Stratoliner'

Manufacturer: Boeing
Status: Operational
Production status/total: 1939/10 built (5 commandeered)

Serial numbers:
42-88623 through 88627

Variants:
C-75-BO: Only identification of the model.

Statistics:
Crew: 5
Cruising Speed: 220 mph
Ceiling: 26,200 feet
Range: 2400 miles

Physical characteristics:
Wingspan: 107 feet, 3 inches
Length: 74 feet, 4 inches
Height: 20 feet, 9 inches
Empty weight: Data not available
Gross weight: Data not available
Maximum payload: Data not available (10 troops)

The Story
The C-75 (company model 307) was an interesting borrow from the airlines for the war mission. There were actually only five of these four-engine machines procured by the Army. After the war, they were completely

---

reconditioned and returned to TWA.

Interestingly, when they were commandeered, their commercial crews were part of the deal and went along with their planes. After all, this was war.

The plane could actually have been called the commercial version of the B-17C. It had a significant data point in technology, being the initial pressurized commercial aircraft.

The C-75, which first flew in 1939, carried four 900 horsepower GR-1820 powerplants. The planes were later modified to carry the more powerful GR-1820-C606 1,200 horsepower versions.

The C-75s were actually the only land-based transatlantic transports in the U.S. arsenal. In order to carry out their lengthy missions, the planes were completely gutted and carried oversized fuel tanks.

On more than one occasion, the planes were fired upon and some sustained battle damage. Fortunately, all were able to complete their missions with no casualties.

Airlifting ammunition was one of the big missions of the C-75s. The planes also supported the British in Libya to hold off Rommel's forces.

C-76 "Caravan"

Manufacturer: Curtiss
Status: Research/production
Production status/total: 1942/25 delivered

Serial Numbers:
42-918 through 928, 6913 through 6917, 86929 through 86937

Variants:
C-76-CK: Given to first 11 prototypes. Carried R-1830-92 1200 horsepower powerplants.
C-76-CS: Five built with only minor changes.
ZC-76-CS: Final configuration of C-76-CS.
YC-76A-CK: Final production model, nine built.
C-76A-CK: Designation given to additional 175 models that were never constructed.

Statistics:
Crew: 3
Cruising Speed: 190 mph
Ceiling: 22,600 feet
Range: 750 miles

Physical Characteristics:
Wingspan: 108 feet
Length: 68 feet, 4 inches
Height: 27 feet, 3 inches
Empty Weight: 18,300 pounds
Gross weight: 28,000 pounds
Maximum payload: 3,000 pounds (21 passengers)

The Story

Early in the 1940s, it was a pretty solid prediction that there would be a shortage in aluminum later in the war. Well, it never happened, but plans were in place to deal with it and the C-76 was one of the reactions.

Since aluminum was a prime material in the building of aircraft, it was decided to step back in time and construct a transport aircraft mostly of molded plywood in order to save aluminum for the combat aircraft.

The interesting program was initiated in 1942 with a plant being built in Kentucky. Sixty-five percent of the aircraft was sub-contracted to the wood industry, with the Mengel Company, Baldwin Piano Company, and Universal Moulded Products Company getting a majority of the work.

The plane was designed to be a slow-speed workhorse for short hops of up to 700 miles. After twenty-five were built, it was decided that the program would be terminated; it had been realized that the projected aluminum shortage would not take place. The plane never did enter service.

An additional one hundred and seventy-five C-76s had been planned, but they were never built.

C-77 "Airmaster"

Manufacturer: Cessna
Status: Operational
Production period/total: 1942/13 commandeered

Serial numbers:
42-38290, 46637 through 46639 (UC-77); 38292 through 38295 (UC-77A); 78021 and 78025 (UC-77B); 78023 and 78024 and 97412 (UC-77D)

Variants:
UC-77: Four impressed Model DC.6 four-seaters, with a 300 horsepower Wright R-975 (J6).
UC-77A: Four model DC.6B Scout four-seaters, with a 250 horsepower R-760 (J6-7) engine.
UC-77B: Two Model C34 four-seaters, with 145 horsepower R-500 engine.
UC-77C: Reserved for one Model C37 which was impressed as a UC-77D.
UC-77D: Three Model C37 four-seaters, with a 145 horsepower R-500 engine.

Statistics:
Crew: 1
Cruising speed: 120 mph
Service ceiling: 20,000 feet
Range: 720 miles

Physical characteristics:
Wingspan: 41 feet
Length: 28 feet, 1 inch
Height: 7 feet, 8 inches
Empty weight: 1,871 pounds
Gross weight: 3,100 pounds
Maximum payload: 1,300 pounds (3 passengers)

The Story

Not much of a story here. Thirteen of these light planes were commandeered for use during the war. Though they were different models, they all carried the same UC-77 designation.

During the war, the Airmasters were stripped down to bare minimum weight and used for photo survey by the 16th Photo Squadron.

C-78 "Bobcat"

Manufacturer: Cessna
Status: Operational
Production period/total: 1942 and 1943/3,504 total–3,487 bought, 17 commandeered

Serial numbers:
42-58110 through 58450, (UC-78); 38276 through 38278, 38374 through 38379, 43844, 97033 through 97039 (UC-78A); 39158 through 39346, 71465 through 72104 (UC-78B); 14031 through 14166, 72105 through 72164, 13900 through 14030 (UC-78C)
43-7281 through 7853, 31763 through 32112 (UC-78); 7854 through 8180, 32113 through 32762 (UC-78B)

Variants:
UC-78: Five-seater, powered by two 225 horsepower Jacobs R-775-9, 1354 built, 67 diverted to U.S. Navy as JRC-1.
UC-78A: Seventeen impressed Model T50, with UC-78 engine.
UC-78B: Originally designated AT-17B, with wooden propellers and reduced weight, 1806 built.

UC-78C: Originally designated AT-17D, same as AT-17B but with some equipment changes, 131 AT-17Ds redesignated as UC-78C and another 196 built to UC-78C specifications.

Statistics:
Crew: 2
Cruising speed: 175 mph
Service ceiling: 22,000 feet
Range: 750 miles

Physical characteristics:
Wingspan: 41 feet, 11 inches
Length: 32 feet, 9 inches
Height: 9 feet, 11 inches
Empty weight: 3,500 pounds
Gross weight: 5,700 pounds
Maximum payload: 1,500 pounds (3 passengers)

The Story
Though lots of UC-78s were bought and used in the war, all were retired by 1949. The Bobcat was used as a light transport and for some training.

C-79 (No Nickname)

Manufacturer: Junkers
Status: Operational
Production period/total: 1942/1 was given to USAAF by Brazil

Serial numbers:
42-52883

Variants:
C-79: A Junkers Ju 52 trimotor transport, powered by three 800 horsepower BMW R-1690 engines.

Statistics:
Crew: 3
Cruising speed: 157 mph
Service ceiling: 19,500 feet
Range: 690 miles

Physical characteristics:
Wingspan: 95 feet, 11 inches
Length: 62 feet

Height: 14 feet, 10 inches
Empty weight: 14,330 pounds
Gross weight: 24,250 pounds
Maximum payload: approximately 5,000 pounds (16 passengers)

The Story

The government of Brazil gave the USAAF a Junkers Ju 52 as a war prize in May 1942. Designated the C-79, it was evaluated and then put into operational use in Panama. In December 1943, was given to the U.S. Public Roads Administration in Costa Rica.

A German design, the Ju 52 was built in large quantities, with more than 3,500 eventually being built. As a Luftwaffe aircraft, it was used as a bomber, transport, air ambulance and a VIP transport.

C-80 (No Nickname)

Manufacturer: Harlow
Status: Operational
Production status/total: 1938/4 were commandeered

Serial Numbers:
42-53513, 68692, 97040, 97054

Variants:
UC-80: Only designation of the system.

Statistics:
Crew: 1
Cruising speed: 135 mph
Ceiling: 15,500 feet
Range: 500 miles

Physical Characteristics:
Wingspan: 35 feet, 7 inches
Length: 23 feet, 3 inches
Height: 7 feet, 3 inches
Empty weight: 1,700 pounds
Gross weight: 2,600 pounds
Maximum payload: 500 pounds (3 passengers)

The Story
Not much of a story to tell on the C-80 'C' machine. First of all, only four were acquired, again by the common commandeering method. In this case, there were four of the four-seat monoplanes acquired. The planes were identified as PJC-2. A single-engine craft, it was powered by the Warner R-500-1 powerplant, which provided only 145 horsepower.

C-81 'Reliant'

Manufacturer: Stinson-Vultee
Status: Operational
Production status/total: 1936 through 1938/45 commandeered

Serial numbers:
All 42-XXXX serial numbers

Variants:
UC-81-ST: Carried R-680-B6 245 horsepower engine.
UC-81A-ST: Carried R-860-E1 290 horsepower engine.
UC-81B-ST: Carried R-760-E2 350 horsepower engine.
UC-81C-ST: Carried R-680-D5 260 horsepower engine.
UC-81D-ST: Developed for glider tow testing.
UC-81E-ST: Carried R-985 450 horsepower engine.
UC-81F-ST: Carried R-985-SB 450 horsepower engine.

UC-81G-ST: Carried R-760-E1 285 horsepower engine.
UC-81N-ST: Carried R-760-E2 350 horsepower engine.
UC-81J-ST: Carried R-760-E2 350 horsepower engine.
UC-81K-ST: Carried R-680-D5 260 horsepower engine.
UC-81L-ST: Carried R-680-ST 240 horsepower engine.
UC-81M-ST: Carried R-680-E1 690 horsepower engine.
UC-81N-ST: Carried R-680-B6 260 horsepower engine.

Statistics:
Crew: 1
Cruising speed: 120 mph
Ceiling: 14,000 feet
Range: 1,100 miles

C-82 "Packet"

Manufacturer: Fairchild/North American
Status: Operational
Production status/total: 1944 through 1948/220 built

Serial numbers:
44-22959 through 23058
45-57733 through 57832
48-568 through 587

Variants:
XC-82-FA: Prototype with two R-2800-34 engines.
C-82A-FA: Production aircraft with R-2800-85 1100 horsepower engines.
RC-82A-FA: Carried Firestone-built undercarriage units.
XC-82B-FA: Converted to be prototype for follow-on C-119.
C-82N-NT: North American version of C-82.
ZC-82N-NT: The final C-82 configuration.

Statistics:
Crew: 5
Cruising Speed: 190 mph
Ceiling: 28,600 feet
Range: 2,300 feet

Physical Characteristics:
Wingspan: 41 feet, 11 inches
Length: 27 feet, 11 inches
Height: 9 feet, 2 inches
Empty weight: 2,300 pounds
Gross weight: 4,000 pounds
Maximum payload: Not available (4 passengers)

The Story
The UC-81 was a highly-used single-engine high-wing aircraft performing in a number of different missions. The plane was powered by many different powerplants with horsepower ratings varying from 245 to 690.

Physical Characteristics:
Wingspan: 106 feet
Length: 77 feet, 10 inches
Height: 26 feet, 4 inches
Empty weight: 31,300 pounds
Gross weight: 54,000 pounds
Maximum payload: 24,000 pounds (42 troops)

The Story
The original design of this widely-used transport was approved in 1941, the prototype making its first flight in 1944, with the aircraft remaining in the inventory until 1954. There were 219 of the model constructed, 217 of them being built by Fairchild, with the final two by North American. Production was initiated in 1944, and completed in 1948.

One of the unsung heros of World War II, the plane was used in a number of different missions, including towing gliders, evacuating medical casualties, and naturally, as a troop transport.

The C-82, of course, bears a marked similarity to the later C-119 Flying Boxcar which would also have an outstanding career.

The C-82 design was accentuated by its classic twin-boom design, a design that was also used in a sleeker version with the P-38 fighter.

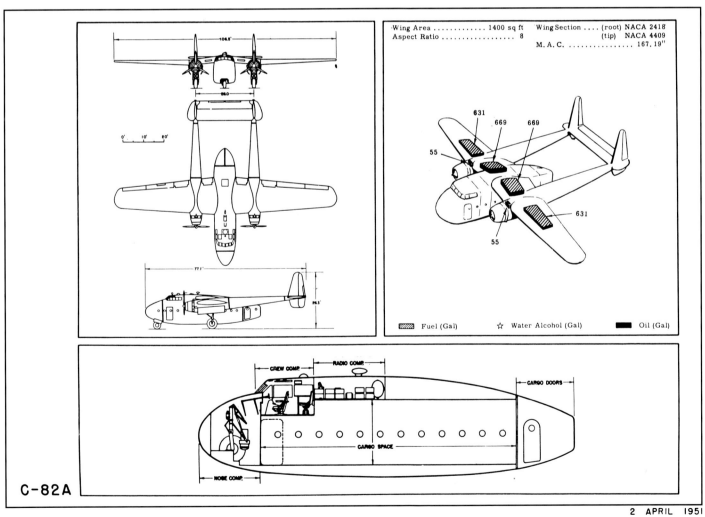

Wing Area . . . . 1400 sq ft
Aspect Ratio 8

Wing Section . . . . (root) NACA 2418
(tip) NACA 4409
M. A. C. . . . . 167.19"

▨ Fuel (Gal)   ☆ Water Alcohol (Gal)   ■ Oil (Gal)

C-82A

THE "C" PLANES

C-83 "Cub Coupe"

Manufacturer: Piper
Status: Operational
Production period/total: 1942/7 commandeered

Serial numbers:
42-79551 through 79554 (UC-83); 79557 and 79559 (UC-83A) and 79555 (UC-83B)

Variants:
UC-83: Designation given to four impressed Model J5A, with 75 horsepower O-170-1 engine.
UC-83A: Given to two impressed J3L-65, with 65 horsepower O-145 engine.
UC-83B: One impressed J-4A.

Statistics:
Crew: 1
Cruising speed: 96 mph

Service ceiling: 12,000 feet
Range: 460 miles

Physical characteristics:
Wingspan: 36 feet, 2 inches
Length: 22 feet, 6 inches
Height: 6 feet, 8 inches
Empty weight: 865 pounds
Gross weight: 1,400 pounds
Maximum payload: 207 pounds (1 passenger)

The Story:
Four Piper Cubs (UC-83s) were commandeered in Panama for use there by the USAAF. The other three Cubs were taken from owners in the States and flown to Panama for use.

It sure didn't pay to own an airplane in the early 1940s, as nearly all aircraft in private hands were commandeered by the government.

In 1943, all seven of the Cubs were redesignated L-4 but remained in Panama.

C-84 (No Nickname)

Manufacturer: Douglas
Status: Operational
Production period/total: 1942, 4 commandeered

Serial numbers:
42-57157, 57511 through 57513
Variants:
C-84: Seized DC-3B, powered by Wright 1,200 horsepower R-1820-71 engines.
See also C-47 to C-53, C-68, C-117, C-129.

Statistics:
Crew: 3
Cruising speed: 198 mph

Service ceiling: 22,750 feet
Range: 1,050 miles

Physical characteristics:
Wingspan: 95 feet
Length: 64 feet, 6 inches
Height: 14 feet, 11 inches
Empty weight: 16,400 pounds
Gross weight: 25,200 pounds
Maximum payload: 3,970 pounds (28 passengers)

The Story
Belonging to TWA, these four DC-3B's were commandeered by the AAF in 1942 and were used for staff transport.

The planes had been built in 1937 and flew with TWA until commandeered.

C-85 "Orion"

Manufacturer: Lockheed
Status: Evaluation
Production period/total: 1942/1 aircraft commandeered

Serial numbers:
42-62601

Variants:
UC-85: Model 902, with Pratt & Whitney, 550 horsepower, R-1340-16.

Statistics:
Crew: 1
Cruising speed: 200 mph
Service ceiling: 22,000 feet
Range: 720 miles

Physical characteristics:
Wingspan: 42 feet, 9 inches
Length: 28 feet, 4 inches
Height: 9 feet, 8 inches
Empty weight: 3,676 pounds
Gross weight: 5,800 pounds
Maximum payload: 742 pounds (up to 5 passengers)

U.S. CARGO AIRCRAFT: 1925-TO THE PRESENT

The Story
Built in 1933 and commandeered in June 1942, the Orion was a transition aircraft from one era of airplanes to the next. Though it was built from wood like airplanes from the early years, it was the first aircraft to successfully use retractable gears. This success allowed a plane with a relatively low horsepower rating to cruise at 200 mph.

It was the last aircraft Lockheed built from wood.

After extensive evaluation, the C-85 was released from AAF use in September 1944. Three years later, in 1947, the Orion crashed in Los Angeles.

C-86 "Forwarder"

Manufacturer: Fairchild
Status: Operational
Production status/total: 1940/9 commandeered

Serial numbers:
42-63350, 66385, 68852, 70861, 78029,78040, 78034, 78043, 94142

Variants:
UC-86-FA: Powered by 175 horsepower L-410 engine.
XUC-86A-FA: Carried 200 horsepower L-440-7 engine.
XUC-86B-FA: Carried 230 horsepower XO-405-7 engine.

Statistics:
Crew: 1
Cruising speed: 110 mph
Ceiling: 17,000 feet
Range: 470 miles

Physical Characteristics:
Wingspan: 36 feet, 4 inches
Length: 23 feet, 9 inches
Height: 7 feet, 3 inches
Empty weight: 1,560 pounds
Gross weight: 2,550 pounds
Maximum payload: 560 pounds (3 passengers)

The Story

Another little 'C' model; it is indeed hard to figure how it got that designation. With only a quarter-ton hauling capability, it is difficult to call the C-86 a transport aircraft.

C-87 'Liberator Express'

Manufacturer: Consolidated
Status: Operational
Production period/total: 1941 through 1944/291 built

Serial Numbers:
41-11000 series, 23000 series, 24000 series
42-107000 series,
43-30000 series
44-39000 series, 44-52000 series

Variants:
C-87-CF: Transport version of B-24D.
C-87A-CF: Engine change and VIP interior.
C-87B-CF: Projected armed version.
C-87C-CO: Transport version of B-24N, never used.

Statistics:
Crew: 5
Cruising Speed: 190 mph
Ceiling: 31,000 feet
Range: 2,900 miles

Physical Characteristics:
Wingspan: 110 feet
Length: 66 feet, 4 inches
Height: 18 feet
Empty weight: 31,900 pounds

Powered by the Ranger L-440 powerplant (which produced a mere 175 horsepower), the model was very similar to the C-61, except for a different powerplant. As was the standard during the war years, all nine C-86 Forwarders were commandeered for military use. Their civilian designation had been F24R-40.

Gross weight: 56,000 pounds
Maximum payload: 12,000 pounds (20 passengers)

The Story

With its huge volume fuselage, the conversion of the B-24 bomber into a transport was a logical decision. A transport variant was first ordered from the Consolidated contractor in 1942, the conversion being made to a B-24D model.

From the outside, it was possible to distinguish the C-87 from its bomber lineage by the fact that there were no gun turrets protruding from the fuselage. In addition, there was also a row of windows in the C-87 fuselage.

In addition to the 276 Liberator Expresses procured for the Army Air Corps, there were also two dozen that made their way to the Royal Air Force. The most famous duty performed by the C-87s was transporting cargo over The Hump in China. A number of those particular C-87s carried forward-firing machine guns for protection.

The C-87A variant carried ten berths for sleeping with six of the models produced in 1943. The model carried R-1830-45 powerplants instead of the earlier R-1830-43.

The most famous of the C-87A models was number 41-24159, which was converted as the first Presidential aircraft, this time for President Roosevelt. It was called the "Guess Where II" and was greatly modified for the Presidential duties. For longer range, it carried larger C-54 fuel tanks.

The C-87B was proposed as an official armed version of the model, but it was never produced. The C-87 designation was reserved for an armed version of the single-tail B-24N, forty-six of which were produced by the end of the war.

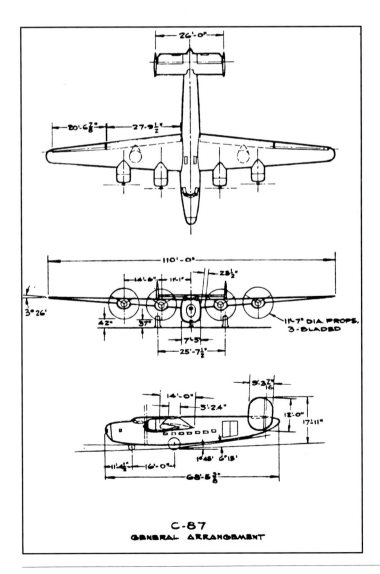

C-87
GENERAL ARRANGEMENT

C-88 "Sedan of the Air"

Manufacturer: Fairchild
Status: Operational
Production status/total: 1936/2 were commandeered

Serial Numbers:
42-68675, 68677

Variants:
UC-88-FA: Only designation given to this model.

Statistics:
Crew: 1
Cruising Speed: 165 mph

Ceiling: 19,000 feet
Range: 1,120 miles

Physical Characteristics:
Wingspan: 39 feet, 6 inches
Length: 30 feet, 3 inches
Height: 8 feet
Empty Weight: 2,300 pounds
Gross Weight: 4,000 pounds
Maximum Payload: 750 pounds (4 passengers)

The Story

A very short story for the C-88, to be sure. Only two of the company model F-45s were commandeered for military use. The model carried a single Wright R-760-E2 powerplant which was rated at 350 horsepower.

C-89 (No Nickname)

Manufacturer: Hamilton
Status: Evaluation
Production period/total: 1942/1 aircraft commandeered

Serial numbers:
42-79546
Variants:
UC-89: Hamilton H.47 with larger engines and extended wingspan. Powered by Pratt & Whitney's 525 horsepower R-1690-5 engine.

Statistics:
Crew: 1
Cruising speed: 121 mph
Service ceiling: 15,000 feet
Range: 600 miles

Physical characteristics:
Wingspan: 54 feet, 5 inches
Length: 34 feet, 8 inches
Height: 9 feet, 4 inches
Empty weight: 3,450 pounds
Gross weight: 5,750 pounds
Maximum payload: 1,290 pounds, or 7 passengers

The Story

The C-89 was originally built as a Hamilton Model H.45 in 1927. Later modified to H.47 standards with a larger engine and extended wingspan, it flew as an airliner in Panama with the Transportes Aéreos Celebert.

After evaluations found the UC-89 unsuitable for use, it was released in August 1943 to its previous owners.

C-90 "Silvaire"

Manufacturer: Luscombe
Status: Operational
Production period/total: 1942/2 aircraft commandeered

Serial numbers:
42-79549 (UC-90A) and 79550 (UC-90)

Variants:
UC-90: Single Model 8B, powered by 65 horsepower O-145-B.
UC-90A: Single Model 8A, powered by 65 horsepower O-170-3.

Statistics:
Crew: 1
Cruising speed: 110 mph

Service ceiling: 15,000 feet
Range: 350 miles

Physical characteristics:
Wingspan: 35 feet
Length: 20 feet
Height: 5 feet, 10 inches
Empty weight: 650 pounds
Gross weight: 1,200 pounds
Maximum payload: approximately 300 pounds (1 passenger)

The Story

Built in 1940, the two Luscombe Model 8's were commandeered and used in Panama by USAAF forces.

C-91 (No Nickname)

Manufacturer: Stinson
Status: Operational
Production period/total: 1942/1 commandeered

Serial numbers:
42-79547

Variants:
C-91: Stinson Model SM.6000A, powered by three Lycoming 215 horsepower R-680-16 engines.

Statistics:
Crew: 1
Cruising speed: 115 mph

Service ceiling: 14,500 feet
Range: 350 miles

Physical characteristics:
Wingspan: 60 feet
Length: 42 feet, 10 inches
Height: 12 feet
Empty weight: 5,670 pounds
Gross weight: 10,100 pounds
Maximum payload: 1,680 pounds (10 passengers)

The Story
Formerly operated by Transportes Aéreos Celebert, the Panamanian airline company, the C-91 was impressed in August 1942. The tri-motor airliner served in Panama for little over one year before it was removed from USAAF service in September 1943.

C-92 (No Nickname)

Manufacturer: Akron-Funk
Status: Operational
Production status/total: 1940/1 was commandeered

Serial numbers:
42-79548

Variants:
UC-92: Only designation given to single model.

Statistics:
Crew: 1
Cruising speed: 100 mph
Ceiling: 15,000 feet
Range: 350 miles

Physical Characteristics:
Wingspan: 35 feet
Length: 21 feet
Height: 6 feet
Empty weight: 800 pounds
Gross weight: 1,350 pounds
Maximum payload: 275 pounds (1 passenger)

The Story
The story of the plane that acquired the C-92 designation is but a tiny piece of 'C' plane history, since only one of the tiny monoplanes served.

The plane was commandeered by the 6th Air Force in Panama for its use. Performance was certainly not one of the highlights of this machine, which was only powered by a 75 horsepower Lycoming GO-145 engine. Its company designation was B-75-L.

Again, it's hard to figure why this plane received a 'C' number since it was capable of toting only 275 pounds.

C-93 "Conestoga"

Manufacturer: Budd
Status: Program canceled
Production status/total: 1942/26 built for civilian use

Serial numbers:
None

Variants:
C-93A: Army Air Force designation.
RB-1: U.S. Navy designation for same model.

Statistics:
Crew: 2
Cruising speed: 165 mph
Ceiling: 15,600 feet
Range: 700 miles

Physical Characteristics:
Wingspan: 100 feet
Length: 68 feet
Height: 31 feet
Empty weight: 20,150 pounds
Gross weight: 33,900 pounds
Maximum payload: 9,500 pounds (24 passengers)

The Story
The C-93 was unique in that it was completely of stainless steel construction and was designed to eventually replace the venerable DC-3. Obviously that never happened, and the Army's intended purchase of six hundred C-93s never took place.

The Army, in fact, canceled the program completely. However, the Navy liked the plane and ordered 26 of the model. The planes never saw operational service, though, and were eventually funnelled into the civilian market.

'Cumbersome' is the best way to describe the C-93 design. The model featured a bulbous front end, and a pair of three-bladed props on Pratt and Whitney R-1830-92 1200 horsepower powerplants.

Production of the plane started in 1943 with the first model delivered in March 1944. That first plane crashed during testing, and the pilot later stated that the plane's durable stainless steel construction saved his life.

The reason for the stainless steel construction in the first place was the expected shortage of aluminum–a situation that never materialized.

In all, 26 of the model were eventually constructed, all of which would be purchased by the Flying Tiger Airlines for civilian cargo use. The planes provided service to Brazil, Mexico and Canada. Several other airlines used the planes into the 1950s, when all records of them were lost.

C-94 "Airmaster"

Manufacturer: Cessna
Status: Operational
Production period/total: 1939 through 1941/3 commandeered

Serial numbers:
42-78018, 78022, and 107400

Variants:
UC-94-CE: Only designation given to model.

Statistics:
Crew: 1
Cruising speed: 160 mph
Ceiling: 19,300 feet
Range: 485 miles

Physical Characteristics:
Wingspan: 34 feet, 2 inches
Length: 24 feet, 8 inches
Height: 7 feet
Empty weight: 1,400 pounds
Gross weight: 2,400 pounds
Maximum payload: Unknown (3 passengers)

The Story
The exact use the C-94 saw during its limited military career is unknown. The plane was civilian model number C-165, and was a monoplane design powered by a 165 horsepower Warner R-500-1 powerplant.

The C-94 was but one of many tiny single-engine aircraft models that were commandeered by the Army to perform a variety of support missions.

C-95 "Grasshopper"

Manufacturer: Taylorcraft
Status: Operational
Production period/total: 1942/1 aircraft commandeered

Serial numbers:
42-79556

Variants:
UC-95: Taylorcraft B165, powered by a Lycoming, 65 horsepower, O-145 engine.

Statistics:
Crew: 1
Cruising speed: 85 mph
Service ceiling: 10,050 feet
Range: 230 miles

Physical characteristics:
Wingspan: 36 feet
Length: 22 feet, 5 inches
Height: 6 feet, 8 inches
Empty weight: 815 pounds
Gross weight: 1,325 pounds
Maximum payload: 215 pounds (1 passenger)

The Story
Only one aircraft ever wore the C-95 designation, a privately owned Taylorcraft B165. The owner, R.D. Maynard, operated the aircraft in Panama, where it was commandeered in late 1942.

Shortly after being taken into USAAF service, it was redesignated the L-2F. It served only two years before being struck from the rolls in December 1944.

C-96 (No Nickname)

Manufacturer: Fairchild
Status: Operational
Production period/total: 1942, 3 were commandeered

Serial numbers:
42-78032, 88617 and 88618

Variants:
UC-96: Fairchild Model FC.2W-2, six-seaters, powered by Pratt & Whitney 450 horsepower R-1340 engine.
See also C-8.

Statistics:
Crew: 1
Cruising speed: 106 mph

Service ceiling: 14,150 feet
Range: 625 miles

Physical characteristics:
Wingspan: 50 feet
Length: 33 feet
Height: 10 feet
Empty weight: 3,130 pounds
Gross weight: 5,500 pounds
Maximum payload: 1,240 pounds (6 passengers)

The Story
Very similar to the C-8, these three Fairchilds (built in 1930) were commandeered in 1942 and used for photo reconnaissance and light transport.

C-97 "Stratofreighter"

Manufacturer: Boeing
Status: Operational
Production period/total: 1943 through 1953/888 bought

Serial numbers:
42-27470 through 27472 (XC-97)
45-59587 through 59592 (YC-97), 59593 through 59595 (C-97A)
48-397 through 423 (C-97A)
49-2589 through 2611 (C-97A)
50-690 through 703 (C-97C)
51-183 through 242 (KC-97E), 243 through 397, 7256 through 7259 (KC-97F), 7260 through 7271 (KC-97G)
52-826 through 938 and 2602 through 2806 (KC-97G)
53-106 through 365, 3815 and 3816 (KC-97G)

Variants:
XC-97: Three prototypes, with four 2,200 horsepower R-3340-23 engines.
YC-97: Same as XC-97, but with four 2,325 horsepower R-4360-57A engines in modified nacelles, revised electrical system and increased fuel capacity. Three built.
YC-97A: Same as YC-97, but with four 3,000 horsepower R-4360-35A engines, enlarged vertical tail surface with provisions for folding, thermal de-icers. Three built.
C-97A: YC-97A's new designation after testing completed, with added AN/APS-42 radar in a chin radome, Hamilton Standard propellers and additional fuel. Forty-seven built, three modified.
JC-97A: C-97A used for temporary testing (48-397).
KC-97A: Three C-97As temporarily converted to tankers, with rear loading doors deleted and a flight refueling boom added (49-2591/92 and 2596). One (49-2596) was later converted to VC-97D.
YC-97B: A converted YC-97A (45-59596), with rear loading doors omitted and an 80-person luxury interior with circular windows added. Be-

came C-97B, then VC-97B, then converted again to VC-97D standards.

C-97C: Same as C-97A, but with strengthened cabin floor and some equipment changes. Fourteen bought.

MC-97C: Alternative designation used for C-97Cs used in evacuating casualties from the Korean War theater of operations.

VC-97D: Three C-97As (49-2593/94 and 2596) converted to flying command posts, with rear loading door permanently locked and provisions for underwing, pylon-mounted fuel tanks. Became C-97D.

C-97D: The redesignation for VC-97B (see YC-97B), and VC-97D, and two C-97As (48-411 and 415) used as passenger transports.

KC-97E: Same as C-97C, but with four 3,500 horsepower R-4360-35C engines, rear cargo door permanently locked, and in-flight refueling boom connected to extra fuselage tanks (60 built).

KC-97F: Same as KC-97E, but with four 3,800 horsepower R-4360-59B engines, and some minor modifications. 159 built.

KC-97G: Same as KC-97F, but intended for use as tankers or transports, two external fuel tanks were mounted on underwing pylons. 592 built.

C-97G: Modified KC-97Gs used exclusively as transports, all refueling equipment was removed. 135 modified.

EC-97G: Three C-97Gs (52-2724, 53-106 and 220) modified for electronic equipment testing.

HC-97G: At least twenty-nine KC-97Gs were temporarily converted to search and rescue standards while Air Force was awaiting delivery of newly ordered HC-130s.

YC-97H: Initial designation for turboprop powered version, became the YC-97J and for a short time was designated the YC-137.

KC-97H: A KC-97F (51-332) converted to probe and drogue refueling configuration.

YC-97H: Two KC-97Gs (52-2693 and 2762) re-engined with four 5,700 horsepower YT34-P-5 engines, used for evaluating these new, very powerful engines.

C-97K: Total of twenty-seven KC-97Gs converted with rear loading doors closed off, extra cabin fuel tanks deleted (but boom still retained) and a passenger interior added, used for Strategic Air Command support missions.

KC-97L: A conversion of 82 KC-97Gs with two J47-GE-25A jet engine pods added on underwing pylons, replacing auxiliary fuel tanks.

Statistics: Not listed as variant
Crew: 5 to 7
Cruising speed: 350 mph
Service ceiling: 30,000 feet
Range: 4,300 miles (without using transfer cells)

Physical characteristics:
Wingspan: 141 feet, 3 inches
Length: 110 feet, 4 inches
Height: 38 feet, 3 inches
Empty weight: 85,000 pounds
Gross weight: 175,000 pounds
Maximum payload: 68,500 pounds (130 passengers)

The Story
As big as the B-29 was, by adding a larger diameter fuselage from a B-50 to the top, the USAAC created the whale-shaped C-97.

Ordered in January 1942 along with the original order for the B-29, the C-97 did not fly until well after the B-29, due to the war-time priority of building bombers first. The XC-97 first flight was November 15, 1944. When it did begin testing, it shocked many with its speed and versatility. On January 9, 1945 it flew from Seattle to Washington, D.C., nonstop, in six hours and four minutes, while carrying ten tons of cargo. Up until then, a similar trip for a cargo of that size took three days!

Boeing had experimented with aerial refueling as early as 1929. The rather primitive method used at that time involved a "donor" aircraft that would unwind a hose that the crew of the "receiver" would grasp from midair and stick into his fuel filler pipe to 'fill 'er up'. The tests were soon stopped, but the idea never died.

Boeing continued their efforts and eventually invented the 'flying boom' still in use today. By creating a kit of the boom and piping, it could be quickly installed in a pod that was attached to the C-97.

During Operation Drip in 1948, Boeing and the Air Material Command tested the feasibility of aerial refueling by using two B-29s. Originally, the competition was directed to test and evaluate a hose-type of system. When that proved to be inadequate, Material Command officials asked Boeing to come up with something else. Dusting off their work from nearly twenty years earlier, Boeing began tests of their flying boom design.

Impressed by the results of these tests, Air Force officials ordered the XC-97 prototype.

On its fabled test mission from Seattle to Washington, D.C. mentioned earlier, the XC-97 averaged 383 mph for the nearly 2,350 mile mission. That speed was 20 mph faster than the top speed of the B-29. Air Force officials were astounded. This large transport was faster than many of the fighters currently in service!

The C-97 flew in the U.S. Air Force and Reserves into the 1970s seeing action in Korea and Vietnam. The last piston-engined plane built by Boeing, it also flew with the Spanish and Israeli Air Forces.

C-98 "Clipper"

Manufacturer: Boeing
Status: Operational
Production period/total: 1938/4 commandeered by Army

Serial Numbers:
42-88622, 88630 through 88632

Variants:
C-98-BO: Only designation for this model.

Statistics:
Crew: 10
Cruising speed: 184 mph
Ceiling: 19,600 feet
Range: 5,200 miles

Physical Characteristics:
Wingspan: 152 feet
Length: 106 feet
Height: 12 feet, 7 inches
Empty weight: 49,600 pounds
Gross weight: 84,000 pounds
Maximum payload: Unknown (74 passengers)

The Story
The C-98 was a majestic machine and would serve as the prototype for the clipper-style transports to follow. The design featured a high-wing configuration sporting four Wright Cyclone R-2600-A2A powerplants, each capable of 1500 horsepower. The C-98 carried the company designation of Model 314A.

The Army commandeered the four C-98s in its possession from Pan American Airlines, but for some unknown reason, one of the planes was returned to Pan Am in 1942. The Army use of the remaining trio was minimal as all three were transferred to the Navy in 1943. With its water-landing and take-off capabilities, its use with the Navy was more compatible.

C-99 (No Nickname)
Manufacturer: Convair
Status: Experimental
Production period/Total: 1943/1 model built

Serial numbers:
43-52436

Variants:
XC-99-CO: Only designation for the model.

Statistics:
Crew: 10 total (two 5-man crews)
Cruising speed: 300 mph

Ceiling: 40,000 feet
Range: 8,000 miles

Physical Characteristics:
Wingspan: 230 feet
Length: 183 feet
Height: 58 feet
Empty weight: 136,000 pounds
Gross weight: 310,000 pounds
Maximum payload: 100,000 pounds (up to 400 passengers)

U.S. CARGO AIRCRAFT: 1925-TO THE PRESENT

The Story

Like the earlier C-87 (which was a transport conversion of the B-24 bomber), the C-99 was a 'C' plane conversion of the giant B-36 bomber.

Only one experimental version of the giant machine was constructed, and it would never make it to operational service. But had the C-99 ever made it, its capabilities would have dwarfed anything before or after it.

The height of the rudder equaled that of a five-story building, and the fuel capacity was over 21,000 gallons. The six R-4360-41 powerplants were mounted in pusher-style and provided an awe-inspiring 21,000 horsepower.

The lone C-99 was delivered in 1946 and did provide some cargo-delivery flights around the country. In 1950, the plane was assigned to Kelly Air Force Base for testing.

Initially, there were problems about how to load and off-load the tremendous bulk of cargo. Over the course of its career, the C-99 set many cargo-carrying world records, many of which would not be broken until the advent of the C-5A.

When the giant 'C' plane was finally retired, she was given the honor she certainly deserved with a display position just off the main runway at Kelly Air Force Base, San Antonio, Texas.

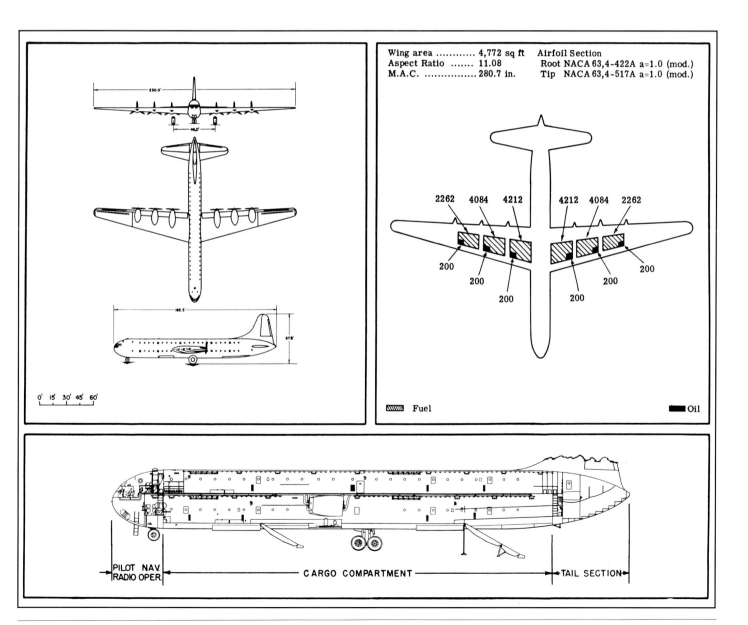

Wing area .... 4,772 sq ft
Aspect Ratio 11.08
M.A.C. .... 280.7 in.

Airfoil Section
Root NACA 63,4-422A a=1.0 (mod.)
Tip NACA 63,4-517A a=1.0 (mod.)

Fuel   Oil

PILOT NAV. RADIO OPER. | CARGO COMPARTMENT | TAIL SECTION

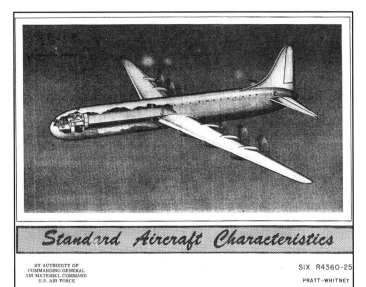

Standard Aircraft Characteristics

BY AUTHORITY OF
COMMANDING GENERAL
AIR MATERIEL COMMAND
U.S. AIR FORCE

SIX R4360-25

PRATT-WHITNEY

POWER PLANT

No. & Model	(6) R 4360-25
Mfr.	Pratt & Whitney
Superch	G.E. BM Turbos
Red. Gear	0.381
Prop Mfr.	Curtiss
Prop Dia.	19.0'
Prop Type	Electric
Model	C-636SP-A
Blade Des.	1129-1C6-24

ENGINE RATINGS

	BHP - RPM - ALT.
T.O:	3000 - 2700 - S.L.
Mil:	3000 - 2700 - 40,000
Nor:	2500 - 2550 - 40,000

CAPACITIES

INSIDE CLEARANCES
UPPER DECK
Length (overall) .... 120.0'
Width (floor level) .... 10.3'
Height (max.) .... 7.5'
LOWER DECK-FORWARD
Length (overall) .... 33.6'
Width (floor level) .... 8.5'
Height (max.) .... 9.58'
LOWER DECK-AFT
Length (overall) .... 40.0'
Width (floor level) .... 8.5'
Height (max.) .... 9.58'
MAIN LOADING DOORS
FORWARD
Length (max.) .... 16.5'
Width (max.) .... 8.5'
AFT
Length (max.) .... 31.5'
Width (max.) .... 8.5'

Mission and Description

The basic mission of the XC-99 is to transport a maximum of personnel, cargo, and/or combat equipment to remote base and return without refueling.

Fittings provided for cargo tie-down include 3000 lb. engine fittings, and 1500 lbs. tie-down rings on a 20 in. or less grid throughout the cargo compartments. A cargo of 16,117 cu ft. with allowable unit floor loadings up to 150 lb. per sq. ft. can be accommodated.

A total of four electrically operated cargo hoists, operating on overhead tracks extending the entire length of each cargo area, are provided on the two decks to facilitate loading and unloading of cargo.

The crew of ten includes pilot, co-pilot, flight engineer, radio operator, and navigator, and a complete relief crew.

Heat anti-icing is provided for the wing, horizontal and vertical tail surfaces. Cabin heating is provided.

Development

Design Initiated: .... June 1942
First Flight: .... Nov. 1947
First Acceptance: .... (Est.) May 1949

DIMENSIONS

Span	230.0'
Length	182.5'
Height	57.9'
Tread	46.0'
Prop Grd. Clearance	4.08'

C A R G O

400	Combat Troops
	or
305	Litters
	plus
35	Attendants
	or
117,000 lb.	Max. Cargo

W E I G H T S

Loading   Gross   L.F.
Empty .... 135,314(A)
Basic .... 138,118(A)
Design .... 265,000 ...... 2.67
Combat *162,250
Max. T.O. ....†300,000
Max. Land....300,000

*For basic mission
†Limited by performance
(A) Actual

F U E L

Location	Tanks	Gal.
Wings, outbd.	2	4524
Wings, center	2	8168
Wings, inbd.	2	8424
	Total	21,116

Spec. AN-F-48
Grade 100/130

OIL

Capacity (gals.) 1200
Spec. AN-0-8

ELECTRONICS

VHF Command AN/ARC-3
Liaison AN/ARC-8
HF Command AN/ARC-9
Auto. Radio Compass.. AN/ARN-11
Manual Radio Comp... AN/ARN-11
Localizer .... RC103 ( )
Glide Path AN/ARN-5A
Marker Beacon RC-193
IFF SCR-695
Loran AN/APN-9
Interphone AN/AIC-3
Radio Altimeter SCR-718
Control Assy. AN/ARA-10
Static Dischargers..... AN/ASA-3

C-100 "Gamma"

Manufacturer: Northrop
Status: Minimal operational use before grounding
Production period/total: 1934/1 model commandeered

Serial numbers:
42-94140

Variants:
UC-100-NO: Only designation given to single model.

Statistics:
Crew: 1
Cruising speed: 210 mph
Ceiling: 24,200 feet
Range: 1,710 miles

Physical Characteristics:
Wingspan: 47 feet, 10 inches
Length: 31 feet, 2 inches
Height: 9 feet
Empty weight: 4,120 pounds
Gross weight: 7,400 pounds
Maximum payload: 890 pounds (1 passenger)

The Story
For some unknown reason, the Army commandeered a single Northrop Company Model 2-D Gamma single-engine aircraft for its use. The plane, which was powered by a 700 horsepower R-1820-15 engine, had originally been purchased by TWA for use as an "Over-weather Experimental Laboratory."

The model looked fast, and it was, since the C-100 had been adapted from the "Skychief" speed plane which had previously set many national speed records.

The plane's career would be a short one. It was grounded in 1943 due to a shortage of spare parts.

C-101 "Vega"

Manufacturer: Lockheed
Status: Operational
Production period/total: 1942/1 impressed

Serial numbers:
42-94148

Variants:
UC-101: Only designation given to this model.
See also C-12, C-17, C-23, C-25 and C-85.

Statistics:
Crew: 1
Cruising speed: 190 mph (max)
Service ceiling: 17,000 feet
Range: 620 miles

Physical characteristics:
Wingspan: 41 feet
Length: 27 feet, 6 inches
Height: 8 feet, 6 inches
Empty weight: 2,565 pounds
Gross weight: 4,750 pounds
Maximum payload: approximately 1,500 pounds (6 passengers)

The Story

Very similar to the early C-12 and C-17, the UC-101 was impressed in 1942 and removed from the rolls in August 1944. Built in 1930, this aircraft was the last of this model produced. The UC-101 was powered by a single 600 horsepower Pratt & Whitney R-1340 engine. The aircraft was used by the Army Corps of Engineers prior to being released. It was destroyed in a 1945 crash in El Paso, Texas.

C-102 "Sportster"

Manufacturer: Rearwin
Status: Operational
Production period/total: 1942/3 commandeered

Serial numbers:
42-97046 and 97047 (C-102), and 107413 (UC-102)

Variants:
C-102: Two Model 900KR, powered by 90 horsepower, R-265-1, redesignated UC-102 in January 1943.
UC-102: Two previous C-102 and one commandeered Model 8135, with a 120 horsepower, R-370 Ken-Royce engine.

Statistics:
Crew: 1
Cruising speed: 113 mph
Service ceiling: 14,800 feet
Range: 510 miles

Physical characteristics:
Wingspan: 35 feet
Length: 22 feet, 3 inches
Height: 6 feet, 10 inches
Empty weight: 870 pounds
Gross weight: 1,480 pounds
Maximum payload: 281 pounds (2 passengers)

THE "C" PLANES

The Story

Little is known about the C-102, other than the fact that three were commandeered. Historical files reveal no details of what the planes did, where they served, or how they performed.

C-103 "Gulfhawk III"

Manufacturer: Grumman
Status: Operational
Production period/total: 1942/2 commandeered

Serial numbers:
42-97044 and 97045

Variants:
UC-103: Only designation given.

Statistics:
Crew: 1
Cruising speed: 200 mph
Service ceiling: 29,000 feet
Range: 720 miles

Physical characteristics:
Wingspan: 32 feet

Length: 23 feet, 5 inches
Height: 8 feet, 9 inches
Empty weight: 3,154 pounds
Gross weight: 4,372 pounds
Maximum payload: approximately 300 pounds (1 passenger)

The Story

The two UC-103 were impressed in 1942. 42-97044 was impressed in November 1942. This Gulfhawk III was powered by a huge 1000 horsepower Wright Cyclone R-1820-G2 engine, while the second impressed Gulfhawk (42-97045) was powered by the slightly smaller 750 horsepower Wright Cyclone R-1820-F-52.

These Gulfhawks were two-seat versions of the F3F-2 fighter, built for the Navy. The second Gulfhawk not only was a flying demonstrator for the Navy, but also was the personal aircraft of LeRoy Grumman. This Gulfhawk was later disposed of in January 1945 and was eventually registered as a civilian aircraft with a serial number of N46110.

During their military service, these two near-fighter Gulfhawks flew from Bolling Field, Washington, D.C., as VIP transports.

C-104 (No Nickname)

Manufacturer: Lockheed
Status: Project canceled
Production period/total: 1943/No production
Serial Numbers:
None

Variants:
None

Statistics:
None available

Physical Characteristics:
None available

The Story

There is no story to tell here because this program was canceled before a prototype was constructed. The program called for the development of a twin-engine monoplane which would carry a pair of Pratt & Whitney R-1830-92 powerplants, each rated at 1200 horsepower.

C-105 (No Nickname)

Manufacturer: Boeing
Status: Research/Operational
Production period/Total: 1943/1 built

Serial numbers:
Unknown

Variants:
XC-105-BO: Only designation of the model.

Statistics:
Crew: 6
Cruising speed: 150 mph
Ceiling: 18,900 feet
Range: 5,100 feet

Physical Characteristics:
Wingspan: 149 feet
Length: 87 feet, 7 inches

Height: 18 feet, 1 inch
Empty weight: 37,700 pounds
Gross weight: 92,000 pounds
Maximum payload: 21,000 pounds (64 passengers)

The Story

The lone C-105 (officially known as the XC-105-BO) was never actually produced, but was born of a modification of the never-to-be XB-15 bomber. The bomber was divested of its offensive weaponry and equipped with cargo loading doors to form this new 'C' plane.

There were several significant firsts with the model. It was the first to carry a 110-volt electrical system driven by an auxiliary power unit. The engines could also be serviced in-flight.

Even though the plane was one-of-a-kind, it still proved to be an effective cargo carrier, being used by the Sixth Air Force for operations in Panama.

Its career was over at the end of the war, when it was disassembled at Kelly Air Force Base, Texas.

C-106 (No Nickname)

Manufacturer: Cessna
Status: Research
Production period/total: 1943/2 built

Serial numbers:
Unknown

Variants:
C-106-CE: Company-owned prototype.
C-106A-CE: Modified fuselage and engines.

Statistics:
Crew: 2
Cruising speed: 170 mph
Ceiling: Unknown
Range: 830 miles

Physical Characteristics:
Wingspan: 64 feet, 8 inches
Length: 51 feet, 2 inches
Height: 11 feet, 4 inches
Empty weight: 9,000 pounds
Gross weight: 14,000 pounds
Maximum payload: Unknown

The Story
With the need for cargo aircraft exploding during the early years of World War II, many research projects were attempted. The C-106 was one program that didn't make it.

There were two prototypes built which investigated use of this model. The first, coined the C-106-CE, was powered by a pair of 600 horsepower R-1340-S3H1 powerplants. The significance of the model was that the entire aircraft was plywood-covered due to the projected shortage of aluminum (which never took place).

There had been initial plans for 500 of the model, but none were ever constructed.

The second prototype was similar to the original model, but there were several changes, including a modified fuselage and the substitution of R-1340-AN-2 powerplants. The horsepower rating, though, was identical at 600 horsepower. The program, due to reported shortage of materials, was also canceled.

C-107 "Skycar"

Manufacturer: Stout
Status: Experimental/evaluation
Production period/total: 1942/1 commandeered for evaluation

Serial numbers:
None registered

Variants:
XC-107: Only designation given to this model.
See also C-65.

Statistics:
Crew: 1
Cruising speed: 118 mph (max)
Service ceiling: not available
Range: not available

Physical characteristics:
Wingspan: 43 feet
Length: 24 feet
Height: unknown
Empty weight: approximately 1,200 pounds
Gross weight: 1,825 pounds
Maximum payload: unknown (1 passenger)

The Story
One of these unique airplanes was commandeered in 1942 for evaluation. Though it was never given a military registration number, the Skycar IIIA flew in the olive drab paint of the USAAF for a short while, powered by a 125 horsepower Lycoming O-290.

C-108 "Flying Fortress"

Manufacturer: Boeing
Status: Evaluation
Production period/total: Four B-17's modified in 1943 for evaluation.

Serial numbers:
41-2593 and 2595
42-66036 and 30190

Variants:
XC-108: Formerly a B-17E (41-2593) converted with all armor removed, armament deleted (except for nose and tailguns), side windows added, seating for 38.
YC-108: Formerly a B-17F (42-6036) converted to executive transport.
XC-108A: Former B-17E (41-2595) fitted with a cargo loading door on port side, all weapons removed.
YC-108A: Formerly B-17F (42-30190) converted as a fuel tanker, all armor and weapons removed.

Statistics:
Crew: 5
Cruising speed: 210 mph
Service ceiling: 36,600 feet
Range: 2,500 miles

Physical characteristics:
Wingspan: 103 feet, 9 inches
Length: 73 feet, 10 inches
Height: 19 feet, 2 inches
Empty weight: 33,279 pounds
Gross weight: 53,000 pounds
Maximum payload: 10,000 pounds (38 passengers)

THE "C" PLANES

The Story

These converted B-17 bombers were an early attempt to force one airframe to do a multitude of tasks. The YC-108 was not successful, for whatever reason. They were never built in numbers.

Probably a major factor was the relatively small cargo area. It was easy to "cube out" before "maxing out," meaning that you could fill the cargo space but still not have a heavy weight–the cargo hold was just too small.

The original XC-108 eventually wound up in the hands of General Douglas MacArthur and was nicknamed "Bataan."

Bataan served as MacArthur's flying headquarters. All the armor plating was removed, as were the bomb racks and the top and belly turrets. The nose and tail guns were retained.

The engines were the original ones installed when they were B-17's– four monster 1,200 horsepower Wright R-1820s.

C-109 (No Nickname)

Manufacturer: Consolidated-Ford
Status: Operational
Production period/total: 1942/208 conversions

Serial numbers:
42-51000 series, 52000 series
44-48000 series, 49000 series

Variants:
XC-109-FO: Prototype for C-109.

Statistics:
Crew: 4
Cruising speed: 300 mph
Ceiling: Unknown
Range: Unknown

Physical Characteristics:
Wingspan: 110 feet
Length: 66 feet, 4 inches
Height: 18 feet
Empty weight: Unknown
Gross weight: 64,000 pounds
Maximum payload: 2,900 gallons of fuel

The Story

The need for a transport aircraft to carry large quantities of fuel presented a problem that a modification of the B-24 could solve. The interesting conversion would be called the C-109 (the B-24 also being modified to the C-87 earlier) and 208 of the model were built.

Ford Motor Company accomplished all the conversions although the basic design was done by Consolidated. The planes were used mostly to carry fuel from India to China to support B-29 operations.

The modification consisted of the addition of seven fuel tanks located in the nose compartment, front and rear bomb bays, side decks, and front deck. Obviously, there were considerable internal changes required to accomplish the new mission.

Fully loaded, the C-109 was a plane that required delicate operations because of the danger of fire and explosions.

The prototype C-109 was a modified B-24E, while the operational conversions were made to B-24J and B-24I models. In another unrelated program, there were a number of B-24Is temporarily modified with the C-109 changes, but the plane's armament was retained and the B-24 designation continued.

C-110 (No Nickname)

Manufacturer: Douglas
Status: Operational
Production period/total: 1944/3 commandeered Douglas DC-5s

Serial numbers:
44-83230 through 83232

Variants:
None

Statistics:
Crew: 2
Cruising speed: 202 mph
Service ceiling: 23,700 feet
Range: 1,150 miles

Physical characteristics:
Wingspan: 78 feet
Length: 62 feet, 6 inches
Height: 19 feet, 10 inches
Empty weight: 13,674 pounds
Gross weight: 21,320 pounds
Maximum payload: 2,355 pounds (22 passengers)

The Story

The three DC-5s were flying in Australia when they were commandeered by the USAAF in March 1945. Only one (44-83232) survived to see VJ Day. In December 1945 it was given to Australian National Airlines.

A total of twelve DC-5 were built by Douglas, first flying in 1939. The DC-5 was innovative in that it was one of the very first tricycle gear large airplanes built (along with Boeings B-29/KC-97 family of airplanes).

The DC-5 was powered by two 1,100 horsepower Wright R-1820 engines.

C-111 "Super Electra"

Manufacturer: Lockheed
Status: Operational
Production period/total: 1937/3 commandeered

Serial numbers:
44-83233 through 83235

Variants:
C-111-LO: Only designation for model.

Statistics:
Crew: 2
Cruising speed: 225 mph

Ceiling: 26,500 feet
Range: 2,000 miles

Physical Characteristics:
Wingspan: 65 feet, 6 inches
Length: 44 feet, 4 inches
Height: 11 feet, 1 inch
Empty weight: 10,750 pounds
Gross weight: 17,500 pounds
Maximum payload: 2,500 pounds (12 passengers)

The Story
The C-111 designation was given to only three Lockheed 14-N transports which were commandeered in Australia in March 1945.

The C-111s carried a pair of 760 horsepower R-1820-F62 powerplants.

C-112 (No Nickname)

Manufacturer: Douglas
Status: Prototype/operational
Production period/total: 1945/1 built

Serial numbers:
45-873

Variant:
XC-112A-DO: Only designation given to model.

Statistics:
Crew: 4
Cruising speed: 280 mph
Ceiling: 30,200 feet
Range: 2,700 miles

Physical Characteristics:
Wingspan: 117 feet, 6 inches
Length: 100 feet, 7 inches
Height: 28 feet, 5 inches
Empty weight: Unknown
Gross weight: 80,500 pounds
Maximum payload: Unknown (48 passengers)

The Story
Only one C-112 was built, its lone purpose being to serve as the prototype for the follow-on C-118 model.

The plane bore a marked similarity to the C-118, and carried four R-2800-34 powerplants, each rated at 2,000 horsepower. The plane underwent considerable flight testing near the end of the war. It was retired from military service in 1949, but would see civilian service for many years. The story of the one-of-a-kind plane ended in 1976 when it was destroyed in a crash.

C-113 (No Nickname)

Manufacturer: Curtiss
Status: Experimental
Production period/total: 1945/1 C-46G modified for experiment and evaluation
Serial numbers:
44-78945 (registered as a C-46G)

Variants:
XC-113: Only designation given.

Statistics:
Crew: 4
Cruising speed: 175 mph
Service ceiling: 24,500 feet
Range: 3,000+ miles

Physical characteristics:
Wingspan: 108 feet
Length: 76 feet, 4 inches
Height: 21 feet, 9 inches
Empty weight: 30,000 pounds
Gross weight: 45,000 pounds
Maximum payload 15,000 pounds

The Story
The XC-113 was born when a single C-46G was modified in 1946 by attaching one General Electric T31-GE-3 turboprop in the starboard nacelle. There are conflicting stories as to what happened after this modification.

There are some documents that say the aircraft never flew and the program ended in 1946. Others say that the aircraft flew until being grounded in 1948. Either way, the XC-113 was retired from the inventory in 1949.

XC-114 (No Nickname)

Manufacturer: Douglas
Status: Experimental
Production period/total: 1945/1 C-54G modified

Serial numbers:
45-874 (registered as a C-54G)

Variants:
XC-114: Only designation given.
See also C-54, C-115, C-116.

Statistics:
Crew: 4
Cruising speed: 295 mph
Service ceiling: 25,600 feet
Range: 1,767 miles

Physical characteristics:
Wingspan: 117 feet, 6 inches
Length: 100 feet, 7 inches
Height: 27 feet, 6 inches
Empty weight: approximately 40,000 pounds
Gross weight: 81,000 pounds
Maximum payload: 17,642 pounds (48 passengers)

The Story
The XC-114 aircraft was a C-54G re-engined with four 1,620 horsepower Allison V-170-131 engines. The program was canceled after the aircraft was built. It is unknown whether or not it ever flew.

Canadair eventually did build a C-54 with new engines–the Merlin 626 engines–and the aircraft was marketed to civilian users as the DC-4M North Star.

XC-115 (No Nickname)

Manufacturer: Douglas
Status: Experimental project, never built
Production period/total: n/a

Serial numbers:
n/a

Variants:
XC-115: Only designation given.
See also C-54, C-114, C-116.

Statistics:
Crew: n/a
Cruising speed: n/a

Service ceiling: n/a
Range: n/a

Physical characteristics:
Wingspan: n/a
Length: n/a
Height: n/a
Empty weight: n/a
Gross weight: n/a
Maximum payload: n/a

The Story
The XC-115 was envisioned as a C-54 with four greatly improved and more powerful engines. The plan was to install four Packard 1,650 horsepower V-1650-209 engines. The project was canceled before any conversion took place.

C-116 "Skymaster II"

Manufacturer: Douglas
Status: Research program canceled
Production period/total: 1945/One model built

Serial Numbers:
45-875

Variants:
XC-116-DO: Only designation given to single model

Statistics:
Crew: 5
Cruising speed: 260 mph
Ceiling: Unknown
Range: 4,000 miles

Physical Characteristics:
Wingspan: 117 feet, 6 inches
Length: 100 feet, 7 inches
Height: Unknown
Empty weight: Unknown
Gross weight: 81,000 pounds
Maximum payload: 14,000 pounds (48 passengers)

THE "C" PLANES

The Story

Even though its designation number is over twice the C-54's, the C-116 was a close clone to that famous 'C' plane. It was also very similar to the later C-114. The model carried four Allison V-1710 powerplants.

The goal of this post-war development was to take the basic C-54 and increase the range and install thermal de-icers. Some discrepancy exists as to whether one or two of the models were built. One thing is sure–the program was canceled shortly thereafter. New models were coming down the pike that put this C-54 variation out to pasture.

C-117 "Skytrain II"

Manufacturer: Douglas
Status: Operational
Production period/total: 1945/29 were built

Serial numbers:
41-18348, 18384, 18392
42-92873
43-15265, 16097
45-2545 through 2561

Variants:
C-117A-DK: 24-seat transport version.
VC-117A: Modification of C-117A.
SC-117A: Air-sea rescue version.
C-117B-DL: Superchargers deleted.
VC-117B: VIP version.
C-117C-DL: Modified VC-47.
C-117D, LC-117D, TC-117D, VC-117D were all R4D Navy versions.

Statistics:
Crew: 3
Cruising speed: 238 mph
Ceiling: 24,000 feet
Range: 1,600 miles

Physical Characteristics:
Wingspan: 90 feet
Length: 67 feet, 3 inches
Height: 18 feet, 3 inches
Empty weight: 19,300 pounds
Gross weight: 31,000 pounds
Maximum payload: 6,000 pounds (38 passengers)

The Story
It looked like the venerable C-47, but it was much improved. Of the minimal number of the C-117s that were delivered, there were many different missions performed, including air-sea rescue, staff transport, troop carrier and others.

The C-117 was powered by improved Pratt & Whitney 1,200 horsepower powerplants.

C-118 "Liftmaster"

Manufacturer: Douglas
Status: Operational
Production period/total: 1949/101 bought

Serial numbers:
50-1843 and 1844
51-3818 through 3835, 17626 through 17643
53-3223 through 3305
65-12816

66-14467
Others unidentified

Variants:
C-118A-DO: 74 troop version.
MC-118A: Medivac version.
VC-118: Presidential version.
VC-118A: Staff transport version.
C-118B: Ex-R6D-1 Navy version.
VC-118B: Ex-R6D-1Z Navy version.

Statistics:
Crew: 5
Cruising speed: 265 mph
Ceiling: 27,200 feet
Range: 1,000 miles (with max payload)

Physical Characteristics:
Wingspan: 117 feet, 6 inches
Length: 106 feet, 9 inches
Height: 28 feet, 9 inches
Empty weight: 55,130 pounds
Gross weight: 108,000 pounds
Maximum payload: 50,000 pounds (74 troops/60 stretchers)

The Story
The C-118 Liftmaster was a simple modification of the Douglas DC-6A transport. The model performed just as well in military garb as it did in the commercial world. The model was used extensively by both USAF and the Navy, the latter with a R6D designation.

The C-118 was a direct follow-on off the earlier DC-4 model, only with a larger fuselage and more powerful engines. The model was the first MAC aircraft to cross the Atlantic Ocean non-stop. The C-118 was used in many theaters through its long career. In 1964, C-118s were added to MAC aeromedical evacuation units in the United States. They remained in the service until replaced by the modern C-9 versions.

Probably the best-known C-118, though, was the one particular C-118 (the twenty-ninth built) that was converted to be the Presidential aircraft (The Independence) for President Truman. The plane was outfitted for twenty-four passengers or night accommodations for twelve, with an executive stateroom.

VC-118A

Presidential Plane A/C-The Independence (three photos)

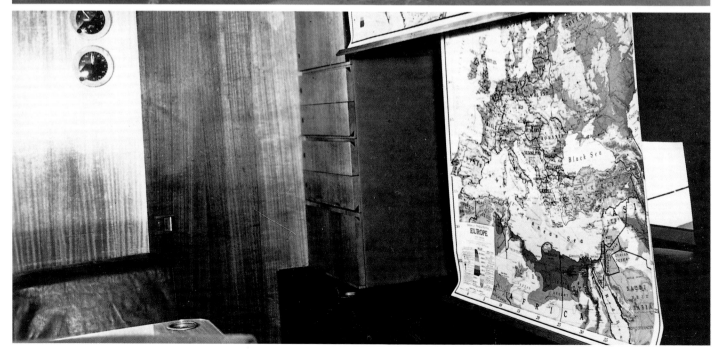

C-119 "Flying Boxcar"

Manufacturer: Fairchild
Status: Operational
Production period/total: 1948 through 1953, 1 converted from XC-82B, 1,051 bought

Serial numbers:
45-57769 (originally a XC-82B, but modified to approximate production standards, became the one C-119A in the inventory.
48-319 through 355 (C-119B)
49-101 through 118 (C-119B), 119 through 199 (C-119C)
50-119 through 171 (C-119C)
51-2532 through 2661, 8233 through 8273 (C-119C) and 2586 (YC-119F), 2668 through 2686 (2687 through 2689 ordered but never delivered), 2707 through 2717, 7968 through 8052, 2690 through 2706, 2662 through 2667 (all C-119F), 8098 through 8168 (Kaiser-built C-119F), and 8053 through 8097 (Fairchild-built C-119G)
52-5840 through 5954, 6000 through 6058, 9981 and 9982 (all C-119G)
53-3136 through 3222, 4637 through 4662, 7826 through 7884, 8069 through 8156 (all C-119G)

Variants:
XC-119A: modified XC-82B, became C-119A, later EC-119A.
EC-119A: C-119A converted to electronics testbed.
C-119B: Initial production model, with two 3,500 horsepower R-4360-20 engines, 14 inch wider fuselage, four-bladed propellers, and strengthened airframe. 55 built.
C-119C: Same as C-119B, but tailplane extensions outboard of booms omitted, dorsal fins added.
YC-119D: Projected version with three-wheel main undercarriage members and detachable fuselage pod. Initially designated YC-128A.
YC-119E: Project only, same as YC-119D, but two 3,500 horsepower, R-3350 engines. Was designated YC-128B.
YC-119F: As C-119C, but with two 3,500 horsepower, R-3350-85 engines. One built.
C-119F: Production model, retrofitted ventral fins, total of 141 built.
C-119F-KM: C-119F's built by Kaiser, 71 built with KM suffix.
C-119G: As C-119F, but with Aeroproducts propellers, not Hamilton Standard, and some equipment changes. Many were later retrofitted with Hamilton airscrews. 480 built.
AC-119G: Original "Shadow" gunship conversion of C-119G, with four 7.62 mm waist guns, flare launcher and armor protection, crew of ten, 26 converted (52-5898, 5905, 5907, 5925, 5927, 5938, 5942, 53-3136, 3145, 3170, 3178, 3189,3192, 3205, 7833, 7848, 7851, 7852, 8114, 8115, 8123, 8131, 8155).
YC-119H: Called "Skyvan," it was a converted C-119G with a longer wingspan (148 feet, nearly 40 percent greater area), fuel in two underwing tanks, modified tail surface with extended plan tailplane and two 3,500 horsepower R-3350-85 engines. One converted (51-2585).

C-119J: Total of 62 C-119F and G models converted with a modified rear fuselage incorporating an in-flight openable door.
EC-119J: A C-119J conversion used for satellite tracking. At least four were converted (two of which are 52-5884 and 5896).
MC-119J: Designation given to C-119F and G models equipped for medical evacuation missions.
YC-119K: One C-119G re-engined with two 3,700 R-3350-999TC18-EA2 and two 2,850 pounds thrust J85-GE-17 underwing jet engine pods.
C-119K: Five C-119G converted to YC-119K standards and fitted with anti-skid braking systems. Among those converted were 52-5932, 53-3142, 3160.
AC-119K: Called "Stinger," these 26 converted C-119G were first converted to AC-119G standards, then with the addition of two 2,850-pound thrust underwing jet engine pods, two additional 20 mm cannons, improved radar and navigational equipment. Also, many were fitted with three-blade Hamilton Standard propellers. Converted were 52-5864, 5889, 5910, 5911, 5926, 5935, 5940, 5945, 9982, 53-3154, 3156, 3187, 3197, 3211, 7826, 7830, 7831, 7839, 7850, 7854, 7877, 7879, 7883, 8121, 8145, 8148.
C-119L: Twenty-two C-119Gs were upgraded to this final configuration.

Statistics: For C-119C
Crew: 5
Cruising speed: 250 mph
Service ceiling: 31,800 feet
Range: 2,018 miles

Physical characteristics:
Wingspan: 109 feet, 4 inches
Length: 86 feet, 6 inches
Height: 26 feet, 6 inches
Empty weight: 39,942 pounds
Gross weight: 73,150 pounds
Maximum payload: 30,000 pounds (67 passengers)

The Story
This unique airplane looks like a P-38 on steroids! The familiar twin booms enclosed a clam-shell door, which allowed for equipment to be loaded straight in, or vehicles could be driven up a ramp.

The high-wing, twin boom design also meant that the cargo compartment had no obstructions – it was maximized for cargo.

The Boxcar, which some also called the "Packet," was a real workhorse. It performed a variety of missions, ranging from the true transport of people and cargo from one point to another to ground attack. It performed satellite surveillance, medevac, glider tug, and airdrop, and was used by Special Forces for their unique mission.

The Boxcar flew with many flags, not just that of the U.S. Air Force. It also flew in the Marine Corps and Navy, and in the service of other countries, including Brazil, Canada, Ethiopia, India, Taiwan, and South Vietnam.

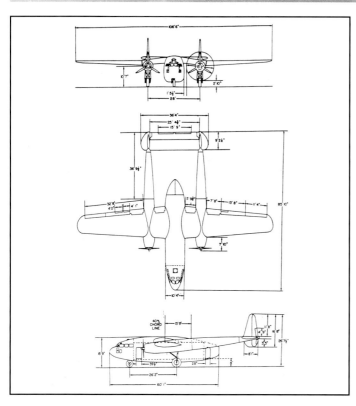

C-121 "Super Constellation"

Manufacturer: Lockheed
Status: Operational
Production period/total: 1948 through 1967, 124 bought, 72 transferred from Navy

Serial numbers:
48-609 through 617 (C-121A)
51-3836 through 3845 (RC-121C)
52-3411 through 3425 (RC-121D)
53-533 through 556, 3398 through 3403, 7885 (ex-Navy R7V-2, became VC-121E, the "Columbine III"), 8157 through 8158 (ex-Navy R7V-2, became YC-121F)
54-151 through 183 (C-121C), 2304 through 2308 (RC-121D), 4048 through 4063 (ex-Navy R7V-1, became C-121G), 4079 (ex-Navy R7V-1, became C-121J)
55-118 through 139 (RC-121D)
67-21471 through 21485 (ex-Navy EC-121K and P, became EC-121R)

Variants:

C-121A: Nine aircraft bought, powered by four 2,500 horsepower R-3350-75 engines. Three were modified as VC-121A, others temporarily designated PC-121A.

VC-121A: Three modified C-121A, converted to staff transport. 48-61- became "Columbine II," the president's aircraft, 48-613 named "Bataan," and 48-614 named "Columbine I." All were eventually brought to VC-121B standards.

VC-121B: C-121A frame, with VIP interior and added fuel capacity. Three C-121A and all three VC-121A brought to this standard.

C-121C: Air Force version of Lockheeds L.1049 Super Constellation, with four 3,500 horsepower, R-3350-34 engines, 33 bought.

EC-121C: Redesignation of RC-121C.

JC-121C: Two C-121C's used as electronics flying test aircraft (54-160, 178), eventually converted to EC-121C.

RC-121C: Ten were built for USAF Air Defense Command as airborne early warning aircraft, with dorsal and ventral radomes. Redesignated as EC-121C.

TC-121C: Nine RC-121Cs used temporarily for airborne early warning training. After training was completed, reverted back to RC-121C designation.

VC-121C: Four C-121C's (54-167/168, 181/182) converted to staff transports.

RC-121D: Same as RC-121C, but with wingtip fuel tanks added and some equipment changes, 72 built.

VC-121E: One ex-Navy R7V-1 transferred to USAF (53-7885), became a presidential transport aircraft, named "Columbine III."

YC-121F: Two ex-Navy R7V-2 given to Air Force, powered by four T34-P-6 engines.

C-121G: Thirty two ex-Navy R7V-1 transferred to Air Force. Powered by four 3,250 horsepower R-3350-91 engines.

TC-121G: Four C-121G's converted to aircrew trainers.

VC-121G: One C-121C (54-4051) used temporarily as a staff transport.

EC-121H: Forty-two ED-121D's fitted with additional electronics equipment to feed data to NORAD ground stations.

C-121J: One ex-Navy R7V-1 (54-4079) was later returned to Navy and eventually became NC-121K.

EC-121J: Two EC-121D (52-3416, 55-137) with additional electronic equipment.

EC-121K: One ex-Navy WV-2, flown for a while as a YEC-121K, the redesignated NC-121K.

JC-121K: A Navy C-121K loaned to Army for testing.

NC-121K: Two Navy EC-121K, one permanently assigned to a test squadron, the other, along with the ex-YEC-121 and C-121J, became NC-121Ks and were flown by VXN-8 for "Project Mapping," a project that mapped the entire Earth's magnetic field. Some early EC-121P were also called NC-121K.

EC-121L: One ex-Navy WV-2E.

EC-121M: One ex-Navy WV-2Q.

EC-121N: One ex-Navy WV-3.

EC-121P: A number of EC-121K fitted with new submarine detection equipment.

JEC-121P: Three EC-121P used for avionics and system testing.

EC-121Q: Four EC-121D converted with new airborne early warning equipment.

EC-121R: Thirty ex-Navy EC-121K and P acquired by Air Force for use in Vietnam as flying relay stations for ground sensors, program called 'Project Igloo White.'

EC-121S: Five C-121C converted to EC-121Q standards.

EC-121T: Fifteen EC-121D, seven EC-121H and one EC-121J converted to electronic reconnaissance platform.

See also C-69

Statistics:
Crew: 5, plus relief crew of 4
Cruising speed: 335 mph
Service ceiling: 25,000 feet
Range: 3,500 miles

Physical characteristics:
Wingspan: 123 feet, 5 inches
Length: 116 feet, 2 inches
Height: 24 feet, nine inches

Empty weight: 73,133 pounds
Gross weight: 133,000 pounds
Maximum payload: 40,000 pounds (106 passengers)

The Story

The "Super Connie" had a very unique shape to it – wings with a definite sweep, four under-wing mounted engines and the three fin tail. The C-121 was an improved C-69, which had been developed several years earlier during World War II.

This version of Conny had many variants signifying its widely diverse missions. These missions included the mundane transportation of troops and cargo, as well as the well-heeled mission of serving as President Truman's Air Force One. The Conny also saw duty as a radar-picket aircraft, early airborne warning, submarine hunter and airborne relay stations.

The C-121 planes were often rebuilt and modified, so a plane built in 1948 might in fact be "newer" than one built ten years later!

C-122 "Avitruc"

Manufacturer: Chase
Status: Operational
Production period/total: 1947 to 1949/1 conversion from YC-18A glider, 11 bought

Serial numbers:
47-641 (YC-18A glider)
48-1369, 1370 (YC-122A)
49-2879 through 2887 (YC-122C)

Variants:
YC-122: One YC-18A glider fitted with two 1,350 horsepower Pratt & Whitney R-2000-101 engines.
YC-122A: Two preproduction versions, with the same engines as YC-122.
YC-122B: One of the preproduction models (48-1370) re-engined with 1,450 horsepower, Wright R-1820-101 engines.
YC-122C: Nine production aircraft, with thirty seats.

Statistics:
Crew: 3
Cruising speed: 175 mph
Service ceiling: 25,000 feet
Range: 2,000 miles (875 miles with max cargo)

Physical characteristics:
Wingspan: 95 feet, 8 inches
Length: 61 feet, 7 inches
Height: 22 feet, 3 inches
Empty weight: 19,000 pounds
Gross weight: 31,000 pounds
Maximum payload: 12,000 pounds (30 passengers)

The Story

The Avitruc were gliders with two big engines strapped underneath the wings. They retained their fixed main gears and retractable nose gear, and were used for only a few years before being retired in 1957.

While they were in service, they were assigned to the 16th and 316th Troop Carrier Groups.

Designed to support Airborne troops, the Avitruc was to bring in combat and engineering equipment into short, rough fields that conventional cargo planes could not use. It could take off or land in well under 1,000 feet.

Though it looked pretty simple, the Avitruc had some high-tech features that were pretty unique for the time. For example, it used reverse pitch propellers to aid in short field landings.

Other features included engines designed to be replaced quickly, with the entire engine able to be removed forward of the firewall using quick disconnects. These mountings could hold one of three different engines (R-1820, R-2000 or R-2180).

Also, each engine nacelle acted as the fuel tank for that engine. With the engine forward of the wing, the rest of the nacelle was used as a 270 gallon fuel tank.

The engine and nacelle were attached to the wing with only four bolts. If removed, the wing retained its clean lines, and could be used as a glider.

C-123 "Provider"

Manufacturer: Fairchild
Status: Operational
Production period/total: 1954, 1955/2 XG-20 gliders converted, 310 built

Serial numbers:

47-786 (XG-20 converted to XC-123), 787 (XG-20 converted to XC-123A)
52-1627 through 1631 (C-123, five only built by Chase)
53-8068 (YC-123D, built by Stroukoff)
54-552 through 715 (C-123B), 2956 (YC-123H)
55-4505 through 4577 (C-123B), 4031 (YC-123E, built by Stroukoff)
56-4355 through 4396 (C-123B)
57-6185 through 6202, 6289 through 6294 (C-123B)

Variants:

XC-123: One XG-20 glider fitted with two, 2,200 horsepower Pratt & Whitney R-2800-23 engines. Original name was Avitruc, as all Chase gliders were called. Changed to Provider when Fairchild began manufacturing these aircraft.

XC-123A: One SG-20 glider fitted with four J47-GE-11 turbojets, in pairs, under each wing.

C-123B: Only production model, with two 2,300 horsepower Pratt R-2800-99W engines, able to carry up to 61 troops or 50 stretchers. Five built by Chase and 302 by Fairchild.

UC-123B: A few C-123B's converted for defoliation and crop destruction in Vietnam. Used by the 12th Air Commando Squadron.

VC-123B: Was projected staff transport version that was not built.

YC-123D: Built by Stroukoff, was similar to C-123B, but had a boundary layer control system made up of suction slots in wing upper surface, improved short take off and landing (STOL) performance.

YC-123E: Also built by Stroukoff, had a modified fin and rudder, redesigned fuselage underside and underwing floats for operations from water. Could also operate from ice and snow with little to no changes.

C-123F: Reserved for a model that was never built.

C-123G: Reserved for a model that was never built.

YC-123H: One prototype built, had an extra wide undercarriage, large, rough field tires and two J57-GE-17 jet engines attached in underwing pods for better STOL performance.

C-123H: Designation given to several C-123B scheduled for conversion to rough field operations.

C-123J: Ten C-123B equipped with two J44-R-3 jet booster engines in wingtip pods, used in Alaska and Newfoundland (54-647, 56-4388/4396).

C-123K: About 183 C-123Bs converted with two 2,850-pound thrust J85-GE-17 jet engines in underwing pods, larger wheels and an anti-skid braking system.

NC-123K: Two C-123K (54-691, 698) converted to armed night reconnaissance and surveillance with sensors in a redesigned nose. Occasionally referred to as AC-123K.

UC-123K: Thirty-four C-123K converted for defoliation missions in Vietnam. These are the famous "Ranch Hand" aircraft.

VC-123K: A single C-123K modified for VIP transport. Used by General Westmoreland in Vietnam. Assigned to the 24th Special Operations Wing. See also C-134.

Statistics: C-123K
Crew: 2 to 4
Cruising speed: 230 mph
Service ceiling: 25,000 feet
Range: 1,500 miles

Physical characteristics:
Wingspan: 110 feet
Length: 76 feet, 3 inches
Height: 34 feet, 1 inch
Empty weight: 31,380 pounds
Gross weight: 60,000 pounds
Maximum payload: 24,000 pounds (61 passengers)

The Story

Probably the only airplane to fly as a glider, a propeller aircraft, and a jet aircraft.

The Provider was based on the similar C-122, converting a glider to a cargo hauler. In addition to hauling cargo, the Provider performed aeromedical evacuation, gunship and defoliation missions in Vietnam. Other versions were used to resupply Distant Early Warning (DEW) Line outposts in arctic regions of Alaska and Northern Canada. The last C-123 was retired from Alaska Air National Guard in 1976.

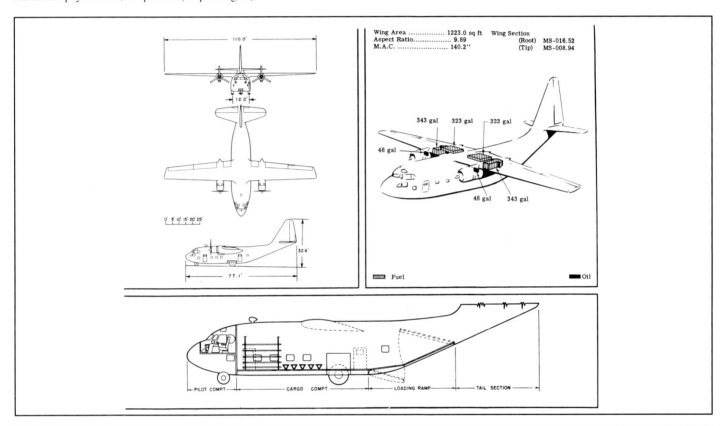

C-124 "Globemaster II"

Manufacturer: Douglas
Status: Operational
Production period/total: 1948 through 1953/448 bought

Serial numbers:
48-795
49-232 through 259
50-83 through 118, 1255 through 1268
51-73 through 182, 5173 through 5213, 7272 through 7285,
52-939 through 1090
53-1 through 52

Variants:
YC-124-DL: Redesigned fuselage, clam-shell door.
YC-124A: Re-engined with four R-4360-35A engines.
C-124A-DL: Production version.

YKC-124-B-DL: Refueling capability added.
YC-124B: Prototype model.
C-124C-DL: Refined version.

Statistics:
Crew: 8
Cruising speed: 235 mph
Ceiling: 20,000 feet
Range: 1,000 miles with 54,000 pound payload

Physical Characteristics:
Wingspan: 174 feet, 2 inches
Length: 130 feet
Height: 48 feet, 3 inches
Empty weight: 101,200 pounds
Gross wight: 194,500 pounds
Maximum payload: 74,000 pounds (200 troops)

The Story

The C-124 was one of the most famous of all the 'C' planes. It was built in huge numbers (448) and served for many years. The plane saw extensive action during the Korean War, the Berlin Air Lift, and finally, the Vietnam War. It basically filled the gap between the C-54 and the C-141 in the 1960s.

"Bulbous" would have to be the best description of the C-124 fuselage, which could carry just about any war material that was in the field.

The huge clam-shell doors and built-in ramp permitted rapid loading and unloading outsized cargo. The plane could also be used as an effective troop carrier.

The C-124 basic design was initiated in November 1947 with the contract approved in April 1948. The first flight took place exactly two years later with the plane officially accepted by the Air Force at the same time. Production was completed in January 1953.

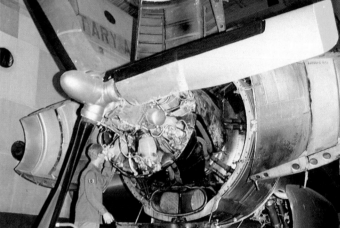

YC-124-DC

C-124C-DC

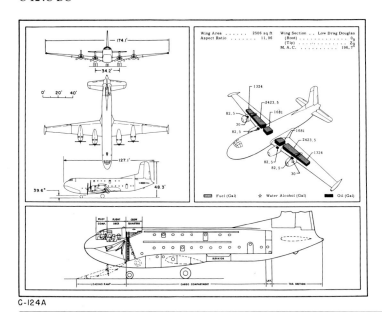

C-124A

C-125 "Raider"

Manufacturer: Northrop
Status: Operational
Production period/total: 1948/23 bought

Serial numbers:
48-628 through 640, 618 through 627

Variants:
YC-125A: Thirty troop version.
YC-125B: Arctic rescue version.

Status:
Crew: 2
Cruising speed: 170 mph
Ceiling: 20,000 feet
Range: 1,850 miles

Physical Characteristics:
Wingspan: 86 feet, 6 inches
Length: 67 feet, 1 inch
Height: 23 feet, 1 inch
Empty weight: 26,700 pounds
Gross weight: 40,900 pounds
Maximum payload: 11,000 pounds (32 passengers)

The Story
The C-125 sure didn't look as macho as its 'Raider' nickname. It looked like a model from an earlier era. The Northrop company model N-23 was a three-engine transport with the center engine mounted on the front of the fuselage.

The plane was designed from scratch for take-off and landing from unimproved fields. An interesting design feature of the C-125 was that it was designed to be towed as a glider to a point where it could proceed under its own power.

Another feature was the jacking tail wheel arrangement which provided a level cargo floor during loading operations.

AN 01-15CAA-1

HANDBOOK

FLIGHT
OPERATING INSTRUCTIONS

USAF SERIES

YC-125A AND YC-125B

AIRCRAFT

This publication replaces AN 01-15CAA-1 dated 19 July 1950

PUBLISHED UNDER AUTHORITY OF THE SECRETARY OF THE AIR FORCE
AND THE CHIEF OF THE BUREAU OF AERONAUTICS

Gartner Printing & Litho Co. — 1000 — 3-16-51

15 JANUARY 1951

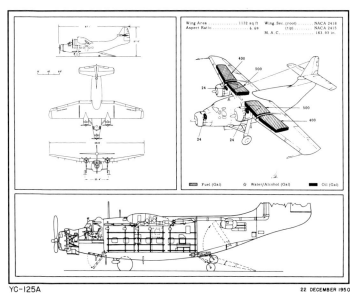

YC-125A

22 DECEMBER 1950

C-126 (No Nickname)

Manufacturer: Cessna
Status: Operational
Production period/total: 1948 through 1951/83 purchased

Serial numbers:
49-1947 through 1954
50-1249 through 1253
51-6314 through 6315
51-6958 through 7018

Variants:
LC-126A: Model procured as company model.
LC-126B: Similar to A model.
LC-126C: Training/liaison version.

Statistics:
Crew: 1
Cruising speed: 180 mph
Ceiling: 18,000 feet
Range: 800 miles

Physical Characteristics:
Wingspan: 36 feet, 2 inches
Length: 27 feet, 4 inches
Height: 9 feet, 8 inches
Empty weight: 2,030 pounds
Gross weight: 3,350 pounds
Maximum payload: 580 pounds (3 passengers)

The Story
One would have to describe the single-engine C-126 as a convenient already-existing company model that met a USAF requirement. The Cessna #195 exactly filled the requirements for use in rescue, instrument training, and liaison duties that the Air Force was seeking.

The initial purchase lot (designated LC-126As) was bought from the manufacturer with no modifications. There were also B and C versions, the latter fulfilling liaison and instrument training duties. The model used the Jacobs R-755 300 horsepower powerplant.

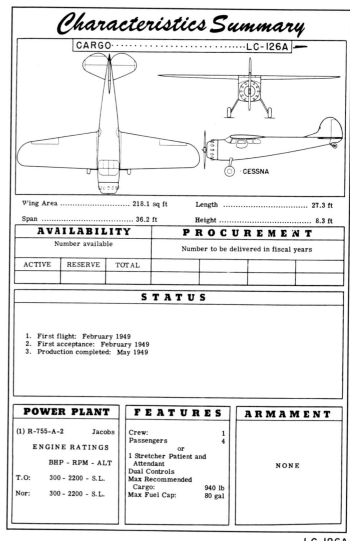

Characteristics Summary

CARGO LC-126A

CESSNA

| Wing Area | 218.1 sq ft | Length | 27.3 ft |
| Span | 36.2 ft | Height | 8.3 ft |

AVAILABILITY			PROCUREMENT			
Number available			Number to be delivered in fiscal years			
ACTIVE	RESERVE	TOTAL				

STATUS

1. First flight: February 1949
2. First acceptance: February 1949
3. Production completed: May 1949

POWER PLANT	FEATURES	ARMAMENT
(1) R-755-A-2 Jacobs	Crew: 1	
ENGINE RATINGS	Passengers 4	
BHP - RPM - ALT	or	
T.O: 300 - 2200 - S.L.	1 Stretcher Patient and Attendant	NONE
Nor: 300 - 2200 - S.L.	Dual Controls	
	Max Recommended Cargo: 940 lb	
	Max Fuel Cap: 80 gal	

LC-126A

C-127 (No Nickname)

Manufacturer: Boeing
Status: Program canceled before production
Production period/total: None produced

Serial numbers:
None

Variants:
None

Statistics:
None

Physical Characteristics:
None

The Story

The proposed C-127 was a promising design concept for the Boeing Company but the concept would never evolve; it was canceled in the early 1950s while it was still on the drawing board. The promise of pure jet-powered transports put the C-127 to bed very early.

The early design drawings bore a marked similarity to the C-124 with the squatty fuselage, majestic tail, and straight wing. The wing attachment was interesting in that it angled down just before touching the fuselage.

The technology was advancing in that the plane was to have carried four turboprop engines as opposed to the reciprocating variety. There also was a swept-wing design that was considered.

A note in passing is that the first C-127 designation was for the DeHavilland-Canada Beaver transport.

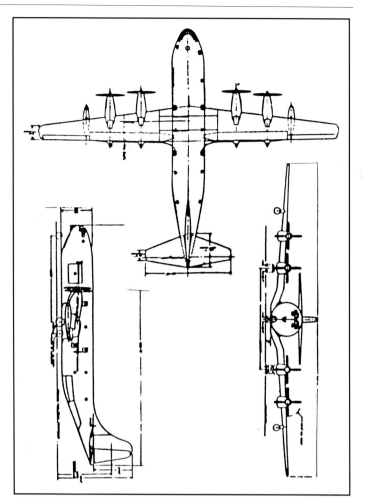

C-128 "Flyer Boxcar"

Manufacturer: Fairchild
Status: Operational, but redesignated YC-119D and YC-119E.
Production period/total: see C-119

Serial numbers:
See C-119.

Variants:
See C-119, C-120.

Statistics:
See C-119.

Physical characteristics:
See C-119.

The Story

Initially planned as a variation of the C-119, the aircraft were instead given the C-119 D and E designations. The C-128 designation was not assigned to another aircraft.

THE "C" PLANES

C-129 (No Nickname)

Manufacturer: Douglas
Status: Test and evaluation
Production period/total: 1951/1 converted from a 1941-built C-47

Serial numbers:
51-3817 (originally a C-47, 41-18656)

Variants:
See also C-47 to 53, C-68, C-84, C-117.

Statistics:
Crew: 3
Cruising speed: 200 mph

Service ceiling: 24,000 feet
Range: 1,600 miles

Physical characteristics:
Wingspan: 95 feet, 6 inches
Length: 63 feet, 9 inches
Height: 14 feet, 10 inches
Empty weight: 19,537 pounds
Gross weight: 31,000 pounds
Maximum payload: 6,000 pounds (38 passengers)

The Story
The C-129 began life as a C-47 built in 1941. Later, it was converted to Super DC-3 standards, then modified with a newly—designed wing and Jet Assisted Take-Off (JATO) engines. It was flown as a test aircraft for several years, then was redesignated a YC-47F.

C-130 "Hercules"

Manufacturer: Lockheed
Status: Operational
Production period/totals: 1951 through mid-1990s/more than 1,000 built

Serial numbers:
Serial numbers run from 1953 through the mid-1990s

Variants:
YC-130-LO: Prototype for model.
C-130A-LM: Initial production model.
AC-130A: Gunship version.
DC-130A: Drone director conversion.
CC-130A: Ground instruction version.
JC-130A: Test version.
NC-130A: Test version.
RC-135B: Photo survey version.
C-130B-LM: Improvements over A version.
HC-130B: Search and rescue version.
JC-130B: Test version.
NC-130B: Test version.
SC-130B: Search and rescue version.
VC-130B: Staff transport.
WC-130B: Weather version.
C-130L: Initial version of C-130F.
C-130C-LM: Boundary layer test aircraft.
C-130D-LM: Arctic version.
C-130E-LM: Long range version.
AC-130E: Gunship version.
DC-130E: Drone director version.
DC-130H: Drone director version.
EC-130E: Calibration version.
HC-130E: Search and rescue version.
MC-130E: Missile carrier version.
WC-130E: Weather reconn version.
WC-130H: Weather reconn version.
C-130F: Navy version.
KC-130F: Tanker version.
LC-130F: Navy version.
LC-130H Navy version.
C-130G: Communications relay version.
C-130H-LM: Advanced C-130E.
AC-130H: Gunship version.
HC-130H: Rescue version.
JC-130H: Test version.
KC-130H: Tanker version.
NC-130H: Test version.
WC-130H: Weather reconn version–the "Hurricane Hunters."
C-130J-LM: Advanced C-130E.
C-130K-LM: RAF version.
HC-130N: Additional modifications.
HC-130P: Refueling version.
EC-130Q: Airborne Relay Station.
KC-130R: Tanker version.
LC-130R: Navy version for Arctic operations.
RC-130S: Reconn/special mission version.
AC-130U: Advanced gunship version.

Statistics:
Crew: 5
Cruising speed: 375 mph
Ceiling: 30,000 feet
Range: 4,770 miles

Physical Characteristics:
Wingspan: 132 feet, 7 inches
Length: 97 feet, 9 inches
Height: 38 feet, 3 inches
Empty weight: 72,900 pounds
Gross weight: 155,000 pounds
Maximum payload: 45,000 pounds (92 troops)

The Story

And what a story it is! The C-130 is THE 'C' plane for all times and all missions. With a design that was initiated in the 1950s, the plane (in its many models) is still active and being produced in the 1990s.

The initial production model was the C-130A which carried four Allison T56-A-9/11 turboprops. A total of 219 were ordered. The A model was modified into many different versions, possibly the most interesting being the gunship version. Other versions would also be modified with that awesome firepower capability.

Different versions of the C-130 served well in Southeast Asia, many times landing under enemy fire. The later versions of the C-130 use the quick-loading and unloading 4631 Materials Handling System. There also have been ski-equipped C-130s for winter operations.

As a partial response to the overwhelming role played by the Hercules in Desert Storm, the advanced J version of the C-130 was ordered into production in the early 1990s. A majority of the C-130s are currently manned by Air Force Reserve crews.

BC-130N

AC-130

AC-130 Interior details

AC-130 Guns

Combat Talon II version

AC-130

MC-130H Cold testing at Eglin AFB

MC-130H Combat Talon II

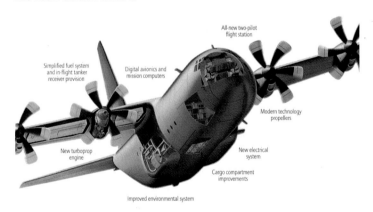

Simplified fuel system
and in-flight tanker
receiver provision

Digital avionics and
mission computers

All-new two-pilot
flight station

Modern technology
propellers

New turboprop
engine

New electrical
system

Cargo compartment
improvements

Improved environmental system

The new J model of the C-130 Hercules airlifter.

It looks just like a C-130.
Until you open it up.

The C-130 is new on the inside. The J model will set a new tactical
air mobility standard for an unpredictable world.

New engines and all-composite six-bladed propellers markedly
improve the J model's takeoff distance, climb rate, cruise altitude and range.

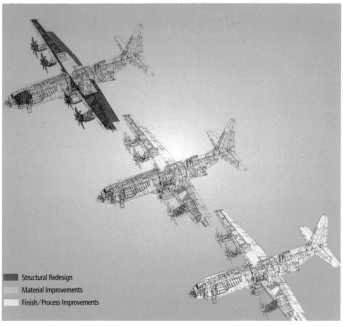

Structural Redesign
Material Improvements
Finish/Process Improvements

C-131 "Samaritan"
Manufacturer: Convair
Status: Operational
Production period/total: 1952 to 1957/112 bought, several others transferred from Navy and Coast Guard to Air Force.

Serial numbers:
52-5781 through 5806 (C-131A)
53-7788 through 7823 (C-131B), 7886 and 7887 (YC-131C)
54-2805 through 2825 C-131D)
55-290 through 301 (C-131D), 4750 through 4759 (C-131E)
57-2548 through 49, 2550 through 2552 (C-131E)

Variants:
C-131A: Version of Convair 240, with two 2,500 horsepower R-2800-99W engines, could carry 38 passengers, 26 built.
HC-131A: Twenty-two C-131As surplussed and transferred to Coast Guard in 1977 and 1978. One later became HC-131H.
MC-131A: Designation given to C-131As when used as medevac transport, could carry 27 litters.
VC-131A: Designation given to C-131A when used as a staff transport.
C-131B: A mix of Convair 240 and 340, seating for 48 passengers, 36 built.
JC-131B: Six C-131Bs modified to track ICBMs. Operated by 6560th Operations Group.
NC-131B: A C-131B (53-7797) used exclusively for testing.
VC-131B: Designation given to C-131B when operated as a staff transport.
YC-131C: Two Convair 340s, with two 3,750 horsepower Allison YT56-A-3 engines.
C-131D: Military version of 340, with Pratt R-2800 engines (same as C-131A), seating for 44 passengers, 33 bought.
VC-131D: Designation given to C-131D when functioning as a staff transport.
C-131E: Convair 440, modified to train electronic countermeasure officers for Strategic Air Command, later became TC-131E. Fifteen purchased by Air Force, two later transferred to U.S. Navy. Also, one C-131D (54-2816) was converted to C-131E.
C-131F: Designation given to ex-Navy R4Y-1.
RC-131F: Six TC-131E converted to photo survey platforms, operated by Air Photographic and Charting Service.
VC-131F: Ex-Navy R4Y-1Z.
C-131G: Ex-Navy R4Y-2

EC-131G: One Navy C-131G modified and used as an electronics trainer.
RC-131G: One TC-131E converted to airways aid checking with Airways and Air Communication Services.
VC-131G: Navy C-131G converted to staff transport.
C-131H: Conversions of three C-131D (54-2815/17, 55-299) and one C-131E (54-2816). All were later redesignated VC-131H, although the former C-131H was informally referred to as an HC-131G. Powered by two Allison T56-A-4 turboprops.
NC-131H: One C-131B (53-7793) converted to Total In-Flight Simulator test aircraft. Involved adding a lengthened nose with its own cockpit, movable control surfaces mounted above and below the wing panel leading edges.

Statistics: C-131B
Crew: 2
Cruising speed: 262 mph
Service ceiling: 27,600 feet
Range: 1,998 miles, max payload

Physical characteristics:
Wingspan: 91 feet, 9 inches
Length: 74 feet, 8 inches
Height: 26 feet, 11 inches
Empty weight: 29,248 pounds
Gross weight: 50,417 pounds
Maximum payload: 9,463 pounds (40 passengers)

The Story
The C-131 was a conversion of the successful Convair 240/340 commercial airliner. The versatile Samaritan was used for a number of missions, from aeromedical evacuation to airway calibration and staff transport.

Probably its most unique and most valuable contributions came from a single aircraft, the NC-131H.

Developed by Cornell Aeronautical Laboratory, the NC-131H had a large, additional nose added the front of the aircraft. Making its first flight on July 8, 1970, the Total In-Flight Simulator (TIFS) aircraft simulated the control movements of large yet-to-be-built jet airliners.

In 1979, the TIFS was fitted with a digital computer and flew for the next six years "flight testing" the space shuttle. In February 1987, TFIS was acquired by Boeing and flight tested flight control computer software and control configurations on what is now the crown jewel of Boeing, the 777 airliner.

NC-131H

C-131A-CO

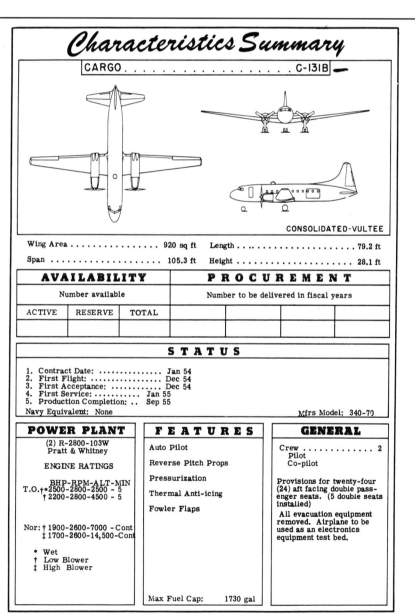

Characteristics Summary

CARGO	C-131B

CONSOLIDATED-VULTEE

Wing Area . . . . 920 sq ft	Length . . . . 79.2 ft
Span . . . . 105.3 ft	Height . . . . 28.1 ft

AVAILABILITY

Number available

ACTIVE	RESERVE	TOTAL

PROCUREMENT

Number to be delivered in fiscal years

STATUS

1. Contract Date: . . . . Jan 54
2. First Flight: . . . . Dec 54
3. First Acceptance: . . . . Dec 54
4. First Service: . . . . Jan 55
5. Production Completion: . . Sep 55

Navy Equivalent: None

Mfrs Model: 340-70

POWER PLANT

(2) R-2800-103W
Pratt & Whitney

ENGINE RATINGS

BHP-RPM-ALT-MIN
T.O.†*2500-2800-2500 - 5
　　† 2200-2800-4500 - 5

Nor: † 1900-2600-7000 - Cont
　　 ‡ 1700-2600-14,500-Cont

* Wet
† Low Blower
‡ High Blower

FEATURES

Auto Pilot

Reverse Pitch Props

Pressurization

Thermal Anti-icing

Fowler Flaps

Max Fuel Cap: 1730 gal

GENERAL

Crew 2
　Pilot
　Co-pilot

Provisions for twenty-four (24) aft facing double passenger seats. (5 double seats installed)

All evacuation equipment removed. Airplane to be used as an electronics equipment test bed.

C-131B

C-132 (No Nickname)

Manufacturer: Douglas
Status: Never built, mock-up constructed
Production period/total: 1952 time period/none built

Serial numbers:
None

Variants:
YC-132: Only designation given to model.

Statistics:
Crew: 4
Cruising speed: 400 mph
Ceiling: 30,500 feet
Range: 3400 miles

Physical Characteristics:
Wingspan: 177 feet, 6 inches
Length: 179 feet, 3 inches
Height: 57 feet, 11 inches
Empty weight: 170,300 pounds
Gross weight: 408,000 pounds
Maximum payload: 100,000 pounds

The Story

This huge transport was a natural progression of prop-powered technology, only in this case those props were to be pushed by turboprop engines. The plane was highlighted by a huge fuselage capable of holding two decks, the top for passengers, and the bottom for cargo. Also of considerable note is that the C-132 sported a swept wing, the first time for a 'C' plane.

But the pure jet transport in the form of the C-135 was just on the horizon, undoubtedly contributing to the decision to put the C-132 down.

No doubt, this would have been one outstanding aircraft if it had been allowed to reach operational status. But pure jet technology had suddenly become the way to go.

EXPERIMENTAL

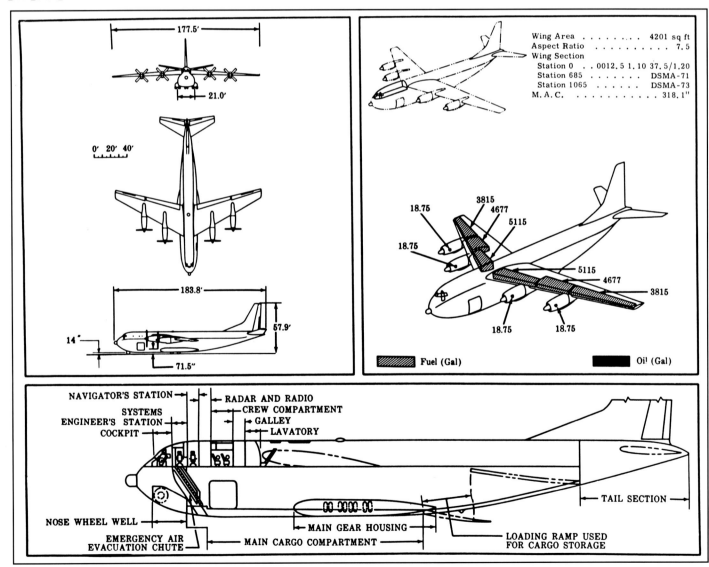

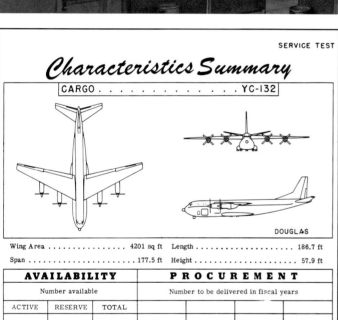

Characteristics Summary

CARGO YC-132

DOUGLAS

Wing Area . . . . 4201 sq ft		Length . . . . 186.7 ft	
Span . . . . 177.5 ft		Height . . . . 57.9 ft	

AVAILABILITY

Number available

ACTIVE	RESERVE	TOTAL

PROCUREMENT

Number to be delivered in fiscal years

STATUS

1. Letter Contract: Dec 52
2. Design Initiated (Phase I): Jan 53
3. Mock-Up: Feb 54

4. Initial Phase II: May 54
5. Phase II: Dec 55
6. First Flight: (est) Jul 59

Navy Equivalent: None

Mfr's Model: 1814

POWER PLANT

(4) YT57-P-1
Pratt & Whitney

ENGINE RATINGS

SLS SHP - LB- *RPM- MIN

T:O: 14,000-4500-6300/9640-5

Mil: 13,500-3500-6200/9540-30

Nor: 11,000-3300-6000/9460-Cont

*First RPM is low pressure
Spool; Second is high pressure

FEATURES

Air Conditioned Flight and
  Cargo Compartments
Thermal Cyclical Anti-Icing
Pressurized Flight Compart-
  ment
Doppler (Air Grd. Pos. Indent)
Emergency Air Evacuation
  Chute
Integral Loading Ramp
Truck-Bed-Height Forward
  Cargo Door
External Pod Type Main
  Gear Housing

Max Fuel Cap: . . . 41,185 gal

GENERAL

Crew (normal) 4

  Pilot
  Co-Pilot
  Navigator
  Systems Engineer
  Relief Crew (3)
  Accommodations (5 extra)

Max Cargo . . . . 195,200 lb

C-133 "Cargomaster"

Manufacturer: Douglas
Status: Operational
Production period/total: 1954 through 1961/45 built

Serial numbers:
54-135 through 146
56-1998 through 20014
57-1610 through 1615
59-522 through 59-536

Variants:
C-133A-DL: Initial version, 35 built
C-133B-DL: Engine change, other improvements

Statistics:
Crew: 4 to 9
Cruising speed: 310 mph
Ceiling: 32,000 feet
Range: 2,200 miles (with 90,000 pound payload)

Physical Characteristics:
Wingspan: 179 feet, 8 inches
Length: 157 feet, 8 inches
Height: 48 feet, 2 inches
Empty weight: 110,900 pounds
Gross weight: 286,000 pounds
Maximum payload: 133,000 pounds (200 troops)

The Story
The giant C-133 was designed from scratch with one major mission in mind, to carry ICBM ballistic missiles to locations around the country, in particular the Atlas missile. The huge plane also established a significant data point in that it was the largest turboprop transport ever built for the Air Force. Each of the powerful Pratt and Whitney T-34 powerplants produced 5,600 pounds of thrust.

The plane set a world's lift record in 1958 when it carried 117,900 pounds to a 10,000 foot altitude. The feat topped the previous record by some 40,000 pounds.

The C-133 was also a significant military equipment hauler, swallowing sixteen loaded jeeps or two 40,000-pound prime movers which could be driven into the giant interior through the plane's rear-loading ramps.

Two C-133s were capable of carrying the equivalent cargo of five C-124s. The 13,000 cubic foot cabin was pressurized to a 10,000 foot altitude which was maintainable to 35,000 feet.

C-134 "Pantobase"

Manufacturer: Stroukoff
Status: Development
Production period/total: 1952 time period/1 modification

Serial numbers:
52-1627

Variants:
YC-134-SA: Only designation of single model.

Statistics:
Crew: 4
Cruising speed: 250 mph
Ceiling: 26,000 feet
Range: 1,600 miles

Physical Characteristics:
Wingspan: 110 feet
Length: 82 feet, 1 inch
Height: 34 feet, 8 inches
Empty weight: 40,400 pounds
Gross weight: 74,700 pounds
Maximum payload: n/a

The Story

There is one single-plane story to tell about the C-134. The plane wasn't even built from scratch, but instead was a modification of the proven C-123 Provider, the B version in this particular case.

The model was designed to test a number of new concepts, including the addition of a boundary layer control system, tail-plane endplates, rede-signed tandem landing gear, and up-rated 3,500 horsepower R-3350-89A powerplants.

A design goal was to enable the plane to operate in just about every type of terrain including sand, water, swamp, and ice and snow.

There were plans for three additional planes, but the order was never carried out, and the program passed into oblivion.

C-135 "Stratolifter"

Manufacturer: Boeing
Status: Operational
Production period/totals: 1954 to 1962 time period/850 built

Serial Numbers:
55-0000, 56-0000, 57-0000, 58-0000, 59-0000, 60-0000, 61-0000, 62-0000, 63-0000, and 64-0000 series

Variants:
KC-135A: Initial tanker version.
C-135A-BN; Cargo/passenger version.
EC-135A: Flying Command Post.
JC-135A: Test version.
JKC-135A: Test version.
NC-135A: Test version.
NKC-135A: Test version.
RC-135A: Photo reconnaissance version.
VC-135A: Staff transport version.
C-135B-BN: Improved powerplants.
KC-135B: Airborne Command Post version.
RC-135B: Electronic reconnaissance version.
VC-135B: Staff Transport version.
WC-135B: Weather reconnaissance version.
EC-135C: Airborne Command Post version.
RC-135C: Modified equipment.
RC-135D: Elongated radar nose.
RC-135E: Equipment changes.
C-135F-BN: French Tanker version.
EC-135G: Equipment changes.
EC-135H: Airborne Command Post.
EC-135J: Airborne Command Post.
EC-135K: TAC Airborne Command Post.
EC-135L: Equipment changes.
RC-135M: Electronic reconnaissance version.
EC-135N: Satellite tracking version.
EC-135P: Command Post conversion.
KC-135Q: Tanker version.
KC-135R: Tanker/reconn version.
RC-135S: Reconnaissance version.

RC-135T: Electronic reconnaissance version.
RC-135U: Electronic reconnaissance version.
RC-135W: Electronic conversion.

Statistics:
Crew: 4
Cruising speed: 600 mph
Ceiling: 50,000 feet
Range: 3,000 miles (with 82,000 pound payload)

Physical Characteristics:
Wingspan: 130 feet, 10 inches
Length: 136 feet, 3 inches
Height: 41 feet, 8 inches
Empty weight: 106,500 pounds
Gross weight: 277,000 pounds
Maximum payload: 82,500 pounds (126 troops)

The Story

The mainstay of the Air Force cargo fleet. That would be a good description, one which the C-135 has enjoyed for many years. The plane first flew in 1954 and has been a critical part of the cargo mission ever since. But it goes without saying that the venerable C-135 has done just about everything else in support missions too.

One of the interesting aspects of this 'C' plane is the fact that a modification of the basic model (the KC-135 tanker version) became the predominant variant of the model. Some 800 of the tanker version were built, but through the years the model has been modified for just about every mission imaginable.

The diverse jobs have included the likes of flying command posts, weather, reconnaissance, surveillance, research testbeds, staff transports, electronic missions, and a number of other applications. The plane just seems to fit any job that needs performed.

The model also has been procured by a number of countries, proving again the capabilities and respect that the plane has acquired.

The C-135 will continue to perform into the next century, as a number of the tanker versions have been retrofitted with more powerful turbofan engines, greatly increasing their cargo/fuel hauling capabilities.

There is, of course, no telling how long the specially-modified versions will be flying.

Below: KC-135 Radar Testbed A/C

KC-135R

C-135 VIP version

EC-135 Front

OC 135

707A Marcer/Transport version

C-136 (No Nickname)

Manufacturer: Fairchild
Status: Project canceled
Production period/total: None/none built

Serial numbers:
None

Variants:
YC-136: Only designation given to model.

Statistics:
None available.

Physical Characteristics:
None available, but very similar to C-123B.

The Story
Not much of a story to tell with the C-136, actually the YC-136 designation. The plane was to be an improved version of the C-123B Provider, but the program was canceled early in the design stage.

No reason has been determined for the cancellation, but it must be assumed that reason had something to do with the evolution of the jet-powered 'C' plane.

C-137 "Stratoliner"

Manufacturer: Boeing
Status: Operational
Production period/total: Late 1950s, early 1960s/5 built

Serial numbers:
(Years unknown) 06970, 10274, 26000, 27000, 24125

Variants:
VC-137A: Modified 707-153
VC-137B: Converted C-137 models
VC-137C: Final configuration

Statistics:
Crew: About 18
Cruising speed: 530 mph
Ceiling: Above 43,000 feet
Range: 5,000+ miles

Physical Characteristics:
Wingspan: 130 feet, 10 inches
Length: 144 feet, 6 inches
Height: 41 feet, 4 inches
Empty weight: 137,500 pounds
Gross weight: 322,000 pounds
Maximum payload: 26,200 pounds (50 passengers)

U.S. CARGO AIRCRAFT: 1925-TO THE PRESENT

The Story

One of these VC-137s could well be the most famous of the 'C' planes, as it was the Presidential 'Air Force One' for many years. It carried the famous tail number of 27000.

The VC-137 was basically a modified version of the Boeing 707 commercial airliner. It had the same body as the commercial aircraft, but with different interior furnishings and electronic equipment. The interior allowed the President and other government officials to carry out business at altitude anywhere in the world.

The VC-137A first flew in 1959. Three were delivered to the Air Force later that same year. All would later be converted to the C-137B configuration.

The VC-137C was the primary Presidential aircraft. It had internal furnishings similar to the B version and was capable of supporting fifty passengers. The two C models in the inventory carry the 26000 and 27000 serial numbers.

This Presidential aircraft would later be replaced by the Boeing 747 version, designated the VC-25A.

C-139 "Neptune"

Manufacturer: Lockheed
Status: Operational in Navy, but never bought by Air Force
Production period/total: n/a

Serial numbers:
n/a

Variants:
Similar to Navy P2V.

Statistics: U.S. Navy P2V
Crew: up to 7
Cruising speed: 345 mph
Service ceiling: 23,000 feet
Range: 3,685 miles

Physical characteristics:
Wingspan: 103 feet, 10 inches
Length: 91 feet, 8 inches
Height: 29 feet, 4 inches
Empty weight: 49,808 pounds
Gross weight: 79,788 pounds
Maximum payload: n/a

C-140 "Jetstar"

Manufacturer: Lockheed
Status: Operational
Production period/total: 1959 through 1962/16 bought

Serial numbers:
59-5958 through 5962 (C-140A)
61-2488 through 2493 (VC-140B)
62-4179 through 4201 (C-140B)

Variants:
C-140A: With four Bristol Siddeley Orpheus turbojets, each rated at 4,840 pounds thrust. Used for high-speed NAVAID calibration aircraft. Five bought.
C-140B: A passenger carrying version, with 13 seats and four Pratt & Whitney 3,000 pounds thrust J60-P-5 turbojets. Five delivered.
VC-140B: Same as C-140B, but with VIP seating for eight passengers. Six bought.
Training versions are also called T-40.

Statistics: C-140B
Crew: 2
Cruising speed: 457 mph

Service ceiling: 42,500 feet
Range: 1,675 miles

Physical characteristics:
Wingspan: 54 feet, 5 inches
Length: 60 feet, 6 inches
Height: 20 feet, 6 inches
Empty weight: 20,553 pounds
Gross weight: 40,470 pounds
Maximum payload: 3,000 pounds (13 passengers)

The Story
The original competition, for a UC-X aircraft, called for a jet-powered utility aircraft for airway and air communication checks, transport, crew readiness training and other assigned duties.

The C-140 Jetstar was one of the smallest four-engined jet-powered utility aircraft ever built. The first batch of Jetstars, the C-140A, were used by Air Force Communications Service to check navigation aids and communications at U.S. bases throughout the world.

The VIP versions, the VC-140B, were operated by the 89th Military Airlift Wing, Andrews AFB, Maryland, as carriers for many top military and government officials.

Characteristics Summary

CARGO C-140B

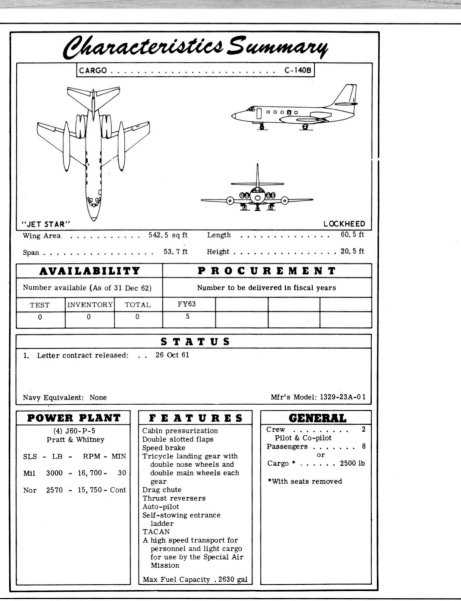

"JET STAR"   LOCKHEED

Wing Area	542.5 sq ft	Length	60.5 ft
Span	53.7 ft	Height	20.5 ft

AVAILABILITY

Number available (As of 31 Dec 62)

PROCUREMENT

Number to be delivered in fiscal years

TEST	INVENTORY	TOTAL	FY63			
0	0	0	5			

STATUS

1. Letter contract released: . . 26 Oct 61

Navy Equivalent: None   Mfr's Model: 1329-23A-01

POWER PLANT

(4) J60-P-5
Pratt & Whitney

SLS - LB - RPM - MIN

Mil   3000 - 16,700 - 30

Nor   2570 - 15,750 - Cont

FEATURES

Cabin pressurization
Double slotted flaps
Speed brake
Tricycle landing gear with
  double nose wheels and
  double main wheels each
  gear
Drag chute
Thrust reversers
Auto-pilot
Self-stowing entrance
  ladder
TACAN
A high speed transport for
  personnel and light cargo
  for use by the Special Air
  Mission

Max Fuel Capacity . 2630 gal

GENERAL

Crew 2
  Pilot & Co-pilot
Passengers 8
          or
Cargo * . . . . . . 2500 lb

*With seats removed

C-141 "Starlifter"

Manufacturer: Lockheed
Status: Operational
Production period/total: 1961 to 1962/284 delivered

Serial numbers:
61-2775 to 2779
63-8075 to 8079,
64-609 to 653
65-216 to 261, 9397 to 9414
66-126 to 209, 7944 to 7959
67-1 to 31, 164 to 166

Variants:
C-141A-LM: First version carrying 154 troops.
NC-141A: Development test aircraft.
YC-141B: Stretched version.
C-141B-LM: Operational stretched version.

Statistics:
Crew: 4
Cruising speed: 494 mph
Ceiling: 45,000 feet
Range: 2,500 miles (with maximum payload)

Physical Characteristics (C-141B):
Wingspan: 159 feet, 11 inches
Length: 168 feet, 4 inches
Height: 39 feet, 3 inches
Empty weight: 144,500 pounds
Gross weight: 344,900 pounds
Maximum payload: 94,500 pounds (208 troops)

The Story

When you discuss the longstanding C-141 Starlifter, you are actually talking about two distinctly different aircraft, the C-141A being modified into the more capable C-141B. In earlier days, the B version would have received a different 'C' number, but that practice no longer seems to be.

When the C-141 was first produced in the mid-1960s, it was realized that even though the plane was an excellent transport, it had one major flaw. The plane was volume limited: that is, the plane was filled up with cargo before it had reached its weight limit. The answer was simple, a technique that wasn't all that foreign to transport aircraft–stretch it!

That is exactly what happened to a vast majority of the C-141 fleet, but there were other improvements made to the Starlifter when it was back in the plant. Also added was a universal air refueling probe just aft of the cockpit which greatly increased the range and capability of the planes.

The stretch itself actually consisted of two plugs that were inserted into the fuselage, lengthening the plane by a significant 23 feet and 4 inches, increasing the cargo capability by 2,171 cubic feet.

In the mid-1990s, the C-141 is manned by the active Air Force, the Air Force Reserve, and Air National Guard. The plane was a heavy participant in Operation Desert Storm. During the 1990s, the C-141 was being carefully inspected for possible structural problems. The plane is gradually being retired from service.

C-142 (No Nickname)

Manufacturer: LTV
Status: Experimental
Production period/total: 1962/5 purchased

Serial numbers:
62-5921 through 5925

Variants:
XC-142: Powered by four 2,800 horsepower, T64-GE-1 engines on tandem tilt-wings.

Statistics:
Crew: 3
Cruising speed: 235 mph
Service ceiling: 25,000 feet
Range: 820 miles with max cargo; 3,800 with no cargo.

Physical characteristics:
Wingspan: 67 feet, 6 inches
Length: 58 feet, 2 inches
Height: 25 feet, 8 inches
Empty weight: 23,429 pounds
Gross weight: 43,700 pounds (max)
Maximum payload: 8,000 pounds (32 passengers)

The Story
The tilt-wing XC-142A is the predecessor of the CV-22 Osprey. The XC-142 proved the tilt-wing design was feasible. It was only twenty-five years later than the Department of Defense saw the unique capabilities of this design and began procurement of the CV-22.

Being able to tilt its wings gave the XC-142 the unique capability of taking off vertically, rotating the wings, and then flying at speeds of up to 400 mph to deliver troops or cargo to unprepared areas, in all types of weather.

The engines were linked together through a complex gearing so that a single engine could provide power to all four propellers and the tail rotor.

History was made on September 29, 1964 when the XC-142A made its first flight, in a normal aircraft mode. Only four months later, on January 11, 1965, it completed its first transition flight by taking off vertically, transitioning to forward flight, and landing vertically.

During the Air Force, Navy and Army testing, the XC-142 reportedly flew at speeds ranging from 400 mph to negative 35 mph–flying backwards!

Only one XC-142 remains in existence, at the Air Force Museum in Dayton, Ohio.

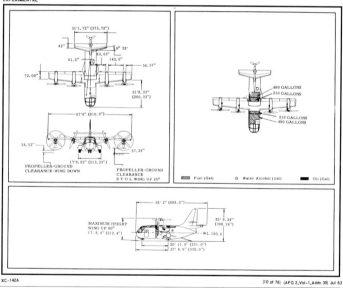

EXPERIMENTAL

XC-142A

(10 of 76) (AFG 2,Vol-1,Addn 30) Jul 63

C-1 "Trader"

Manufacturer: Grumman
Status: Used exclusively by the Navy
Production period/total: 87 built

Serial numbers:
Not available

Variants:
Not available

Statistics:
Crew: 3
Cruising speed: 180 mph; max speed 280 mph
Service ceiling: 22,000 feet
Range: not available

Physical characteristics:
Wingspan: 72 feet, 7 inches
Length: 43 feet, 6 inches
Height: 17 feet, 6 inches
Empty weight: 18,315 pounds
Gross weight: 26,147 pounds
Maximum payload: 3,500 pounds (9 passengers)

C-2 "Greyhound"

Manufacturer: Grumman
Status: Operational, used exclusively by U.S. Navy
Production period/total: 1962 and 1963/19 bought; 1989/39 bought.

Serial numbers:
Bu152786/152797, 155120/155124 (C-2A)

Variants:
C-2A: With two 1,005 horsepower, Lycoming T53-7 turboprops.
C-2 was a conversion of the Grumman E-2 Hawkeye.

Statistics:
Crew: 3
Cruising speed: 299 mph; max 352 mph
Service ceiling: 33,500 feet
Range: 1,700 miles

Physical characteristics:
Wingspan: 80 feet, 7 inches
Length: 57 feet, 7 inches
Height: 15 feet, 11 inches

Empty weight: 31,154 pounds
Gross weight: 54,830 pounds
Maximum payload: 10,000 pounds (off a carrier), 15,000 pounds (off land), or 39 passengers

The Story
C-2A was a transport version of the E-2. By redesigning the fuselage to carry 39 passengers, and matching it to the E-2 wings and engines, the Greyhound was born.

The first C-2 flew in November 1964, preceded by the E-2 by about four years.

The Greyhound came about when the Navy decided they needed an aircraft that could rapidly deliver high priority cargo or people to the U.S. carrier fleet.

Capable of catapult takeoffs and arresting cable landings with 39 passengers or the equivalent in cargo, the Greyhound excelled at COD (Carrier On-board Delivery) work. COD has been an essential, though unsung, cog in the Navy. You won't find Tom Cruise flying a Greyhound, no matter how fast the name may sound.

Seventeen C-2A were bought by the Navy, and an additional order for twelve was canceled. Later, in 1989, another 39 new airframes were purchased.

C-3 "4-0-4"

Manufacturer: Martin
Status: Operational, by Coast Guard, and later, the Navy
Production period/total: 1962/2 bought by Coast Guard

Serial numbers:
Coast Guard registration 1282 and 1283, when transferred to Navy, became Bu158202 and 158203.

Variants:
VC-3: Two RM-1Z bought by USCG, redesignated as VC-3A in 1962.

Statistics:
Crew:
Cruising speed: 280 mph
Service ceiling: 30,000 feet
Range: 1,080-2,600 miles

Physical characteristics:
Wingspan: 93 feet, 3 inches
Length: 74 feet, 7 inches
Height: unknown
Empty weight: approximately 24,000 pounds
Gross weight: 43,650 pounds
Maximum payload: **XXX** pounds, **XXX** passengers

The Story
The Coast Guard bought two Martin 4-0-4 as RM-1Z. Later, in 1962, they were redesignated as VC-3As and transferred to the Navy.

This aircraft was powered by 2,400 horsepower Pratt & Whitney R-2800-CB16 engines.

C-4 "Academe"

Manufacturer: Grumman
Status: Operational
Production period/total: 1962/10 delivered; 1 to USCG, nine to U.S. Navy

Serial numbers:
USCG 1380, and Bu155722/155730

Variants:
VC-4A: One delivered to USCG, with two 2,190 horsepower Rolls-Royce Dart engines.
TC-4B: Projected navigational trainer, with radar in lengthened nose, ten ordered, then canceled.
TC-4C: A-6 Intruder crew trainer, with two 2,185 horsepower Rolls-Royce Dart Mk. 529-LC engines, nine delivered to U.S. Navy.

Statistics:
unknown

Physical characteristics:
unknown

C-5A "Galaxy"

Manufacturer: Lockheed
Status: Operational
Production period/total: Late 1960s, early 1970s/125 built

Serial numbers:
66-8303 through 8307
67-167 through 174
68-211 through 228
69-1 through 27,
70-445 through 467 (C-5A versions)
87-0027 through 0045 (C-5B versions)

Variants:
C-5A: Initial version
C-5B: Second variant which incorporated wing modification (included both modified C-5As and newly-constructed C-5Bs.)

Statistics:
Crew: 5 to 8
Cruising speed: 520 mph
Ceiling: 35,000+ feet
Range: 6,300 miles with 100,000 pound payload

Physical Characteristics:
Wingspan: 222 feet, 9 inches
Length: 247 feet, 10 inches
Height: 65 feet, 1 inch
Empty weight: 325,200 pounds
Gross weight: 712,000 pounds
Maximum payload: 255,000 pounds (Outsized cargo)

The Story

When you first view the C-5 Galaxy, it's frankly quite an overwhelming sight. It can almost fill a football field with its mammoth size, totally dwarfing just about every aircraft in the world.

The plane was designed from scratch to provide massive support for deployment and resupply of combat and support forces. The plane is capable of airlifting every type of Army equipment including tanks, self-propelled artillery, and helicopters. The cargo department ceiling height of 13.5 feet extends the length of the fuselage and large 19-foot wide openings and integral ramps fore and aft permit 'drive through' loading and unloading.

The C-5 prototype first flew in June 1968, with the Air Force taking delivery of the first 81 models between 1969 and 1973.

But all was not roses for the C-5 when, in the mid-1970s, wing crack problems were noted on some of the Galaxies. As a result, it was necessary to accomplish a significant wing fix job back at the Lockheed production facility in Georgia.

The fix (which was accomplished between 1982 and 1987) was successful. The planes have continued to perform in outstanding fashion into the mid-1990s.

The follow-on batch of fifty C-5Bs had the wing modification incorporated along with other improvements. The C-5Bs incorporated the General Electric TF39 powerplants, and updated avionics.

Starting in 1970, the C-5s were used routinely in Southeast Asia, and later would be used in Operation Desert Storm. One of the planes, however, was lost in supporting that latter operation.

In more recent times, the C-5 fleet has been retrofitted with new interior panels. A number of the Galaxies have also been fitted with the Tracor flare dispenser system, and a Honeywell AN/AAR-47 missile warning defense system.

C-6 (No Nickname)

Manufacturer: Beech
Status: Operational
Production period/total: 1960s/1 purchased; in 1980/15 purchased (Spanish AF, FAA)

Serial Numbers:
66-7943 (USAF)

Variants:
VC-6A-BH: Designation of early model.
VC-6B: Spanish Air Force version.

Statistics:
Crew: 2
Cruising speed: 272 mph
Ceiling: 28,100 feet
Range: 6,400 miles

Physical Characteristics:
Wingspan: 50 feet, 3 inches
Length: 35 feet, 6 inches
Height: 14 feet, 3 inches
Empty weight: 5,765 pounds
Gross weight: 9,700 pounds
Maximum payload: Not reported

The Story

There's a very short story to tell about the C-6 designation as far as the Air Force was concerned, since there was only one plane carrying the tag.

Later, though, the Spanish Air Force and FAA would purchase a total of fifteen of the B version of the model.

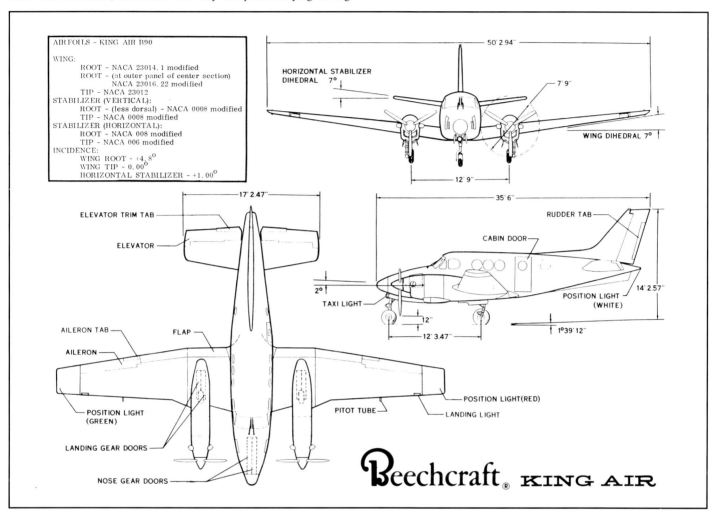

```
AIRFOILS - KING AIR B90

WING:
    ROOT - NACA 23014.1 modified
    ROOT - (at outer panel of center section)
           NACA 23016.22 modified
    TIP - NACA 23012
STABILIZER (VERTICAL):
    ROOT - (less dorsal) - NACA 0008 modified
    TIP - NACA 0008 modified
STABILIZER (HORIZONTAL):
    ROOT - NACA 008 modified
    TIP - NACA 006 modified
INCIDENCE:
    WING ROOT - +4.8°
    WING TIP - 0.00°
    HORIZONTAL STABILIZER - +1.00°
```

Beechcraft® KING AIR

C-7 "Caribou"

Manufacturer: De Havilland Canada
Status: Operational
Production period/total: Late 1950s, early 1960s/330+ built

Serial numbers:
60-3762 through 3768, 5430 through 5444
61-2591 through 2600, 2384 through 2407
62-4144 through 4196, 12583 through 12584
63-7924 through 7971 (all C-7A versions), 9718 through 9765 (B versions)

Variants:
CC-108: RCAF version.
YAC-1: U.S. Army evaluation models.

AC-1: Initial Army operational models.
CV-2A/CV-2B: Army operational designations.
C-7A/C-7B: USAF designations.

Statistics:
Crew: 2
Cruising speed: 216 mph
Ceiling: 24,800 feet
Range: 242 miles (with maximum payload)

Physical Characteristics:
Wingspan: 95 feet, 7 inches
Length: 72 feet, 7 inches
Height: 31 feet, 9 inches
Empty weight: 18,260 pounds
Gross weight: 31,300 pounds
Maximum payload: 8,700 pounds (22 stretchers)

THE "C" PLANES

The Story

The high-wing Caribou was identified with the company designation of DHC-4. It was first flown in July 1958, with service evaluation taking place in August 1959. First deliveries took place in 1961.

The initial evaluation was accomplished by the Royal Canadian Air Force (RCAF) with the model designated as the CC-108. The U.S. Army then accomplished its own evaluation with five of the models, and then took delivery of five of the models in the early 1960s. The Army give the models two designations, C-7A and C-7B. The planes provided heavy support in Southeast Asia.

The plane received high marks for its performance and was produced for a dozen other countries, in addition to a number of civilian organizations and the United Nations.

The main attributes of the Caribou were its short field capability and the ability to operate from extremely rough and unimproved fields.

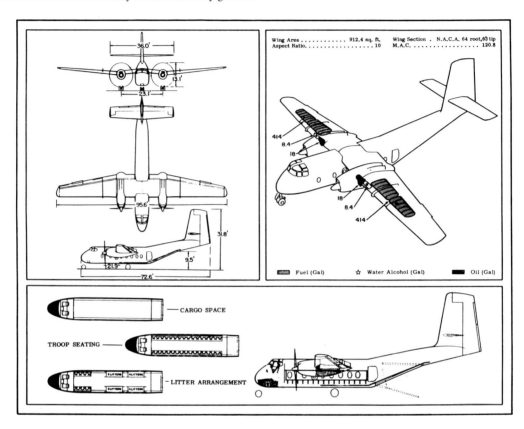

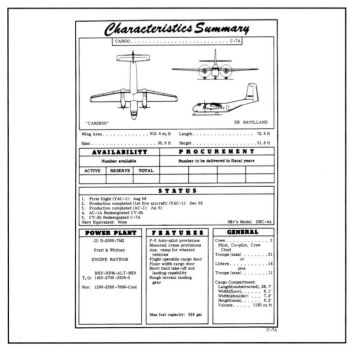

C-8 "Buffalo"

Manufacturer: De Havilland, Canada
Status: Operational
Production period/total: Mid-1960s/4 built for U.S. Army

Serial numbers:
Not available

Variants:
C-8A: Only designation given to this model.

Statistics:
Crew: 2
Cruising speed: 271 mph
Ceiling: 30,000 feet
Range: 507 miles with maximum payload

Physical Characteristics:
Wingspan: 96 feet
Length: 77 feet, 4 inches
Height: 28 feet, 8 inches
Empty weight: 23,160 pounds

Gross weight: 41,000 pounds
Maximum payload: 13,800 pounds (41 troops)

The Story
Quite similar to the earlier C-7A, the C-8A Buffalo was designed from scratch to be a STOL tactical transport. The competition was won against two dozen other competitors. The goal was to build a transport for U.S. Army requirements.

The model featured a high-wing design, carried a pair of 2,850 horsepower General Electric turboprop engines, and sported a T-tail.

Financially, the program was actually a three-fold situation; the costs were shared by the company, the Army, and the Canadian government. The Army evaluated four of the C-8As, but for some unknown reason, the U.S. decided to cancel its participation in the program.

The Canadian government, though, felt differently about the program and purchased fifteen of the models. The Canadian version was called the CC-115 and there were slight differences from the C-8A version. Later, Peru bought sixteen and Brazil purchased twenty-four of the STOL transports, pushing the final production total to 59.

There would, however, be one final U.S. involvement with a joint program attempting the development of an air-cushion landing system on a modified C-8A.

C-9 "Nightingale" or "Skytrain II"

Manufacturer: McDonnell Douglas
Status: Operational
Production period/total: 1967 to 1973/23 for USAF, 16 for USN

Serial numbers:
67-22583 through 2258
68-8932 through 8935, 10958 through 10961
71-874 through 882 (all C-9A-DL)
Bu159113 through Bu1159120
Bu1160046 through Bu1160051 (all C-9B-DL)
73-1681 through 1683 (all VC-9C-DL)
Bu1607749 through Bu1160750 (all C-9K-DL)

Variants:
C-9A-DL: Initial version, twenty purchased by USAF for medical evacuation use.
C-9B-DL: U.S. Navy version, fourteen delivered.
VC-9C-DL: Three models modified for executive use.
C-9K-DL: Kuwaiti Air Force version.

Statistics:
Crew: 8
Cruising speed: 565 mph
Ceiling: 35,000 feet
Range: 2,000+ miles

Physical Characteristics:
Wingspan: 93 feet, 3 inches
Length: 119 feet, 3 inches
Height: 27 feet, 5 inches
Empty weight: 57,190 pounds
Gross weight: 121,000 pounds
Maximum payload: 10,000+ pounds (40 litter patients)

The Story
The need was definite in the mid-1960s for a new, highly efficient aeromedevac transport. The existing C-118 was no longer able to fulfill the required missions, so the Air Force turned to a commercial development (the existing DC-9) to accomplish the important mission. It was decided that the Series 30 model would exactly fulfill the requirements.

The military versions were equipped with two Pratt & Whitney 14,500 pound JT8D-9 turbofans. Needless to say, the interiors of these transports were radically changed for the medical missions. The changes provided for forty stretcher patients, with an even greater number of patients being accommodated in regular seats. There also were special accommodations that could be used for seriously injured patients.

The C-9B version was a refined version of the original and was used by the Navy. The Navy version was given the nickname of "Skytrain II." There also was a VIP version of the C-9B, called the VC-9B, that was ordered in minimal numbers.

The Nightingale was still serving in the mid-1990s.

C-10 "Jetstream"

Manufacturer: Handley Page
Status: Ordered, but later canceled
Production period/total: 1968/11 ordered, 4 on option, all eventually canceled

Serial numbers:
68-10378 through 10388 (ordered), 10389 through 10392 (options)

Variants:
C-10A: Jetstream 31, powered by two Garrett-AiResearch TPE-33-301W turboprops, with strengthened floor and larger cargo door.

Statistics:
Crew: 2
Cruising speed: 282 mph (max)
Service ceiling: undetermined
Range: 1,380 miles

Physical characteristics:

Wingspan: 52 feet
Length: 47 feet, 1 inch
Height: unknown
Empty weight: approximately 8,000 pounds
Gross weight: 12,566 pounds
Maximum payload: approximately 2,000 pounds (4 passengers)

The Story

The Jetstream was to be a conversion of Britain's Handley Page Model 137, the Jetstream 31. It was powered by turboprops from the American company of Garret-AiResearch.

The initial order and options were canceled in October 1969 because Handley Page was unable to meet the specified delivery dates, due to severe financial problems.

In an unusual move, the Air Force put the designation C-10 back into the system, and McDonnell Douglas DC-10s were later given this designation.

Above: **C-10**

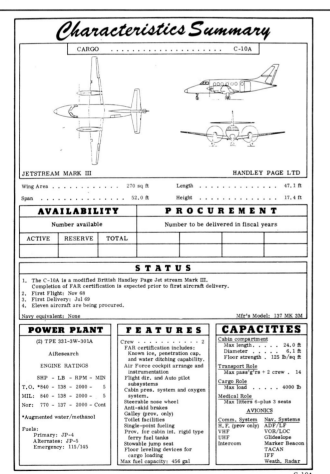

Characteristics Summary

CARGO	. . . .	C-10A

JETSTREAM MARK III   HANDLEY PAGE LTD

Wing Area	270 sq ft	Length	47.1 ft
Span	52.0 ft	Height	17.4 ft

AVAILABILITY			PROCUREMENT		
Number available			Number to be delivered in fiscal years		
ACTIVE	RESERVE	TOTAL			

STATUS

1. The C-10A is a modified British Handley Page Jet stream Mark III. Completion of FAR certification is expected prior to first aircraft delivery.
2. First Flight: Nov 68
3. First Delivery: Jul 69
4. Eleven aircraft are being procured.

Navy equivalent: None   Mfr's Model: 137 MK 3M

POWER PLANT	FEATURES	CAPACITIES

(2) TPE 331-3W-301A
 	
AiResearch
 	
ENGINE RATINGS
 	
SHP - LB - RPM - MIN
 	
T.O. *840 - 138 - 2000 - 5
MIL: 840 - 138 - 2000 - 5
Nor: 770 - 137 - 2000 - Cont
 	
*Augmented water/methanol
 	
Fuels:
  Primary: JP-4
  Alternates: JP-5
  Emergency: 115/145
	Crew 2
	FAR certification includes:
	  Known ice, penetration cap.
	  and water ditching capability.
	Air Force cockpit arrange and
	  instrumentation
	Flight dir. and Auto pilot
	  subsystems
	Cabin pres. system and oxygen
	  system.
	Steerable nose wheel
	Anti-skid brakes
	Galley (prov. only)
	Toilet facilities
	Single-point fueling
	Prov. for cabin int. rigid type
	  ferry fuel tanks
	Stowable jump seat
	Floor leveling devices for
	  cargo loading
	Max fuel capacity: 456 gal
		Cabin compartment
		  Max length . . . . 24.0 ft
		  Diameter . . . . . 6.1 ft
		  Floor strength . 125 lb/sq ft
		Transport Role
		  Max pass'g'rs + 2 crew . 14
		Cargo Role
		  Max load . . . . . 4000 lb
		Medical Role
		  Max litters 6-plus 3 seats
		AVIONICS
		Comm. System Nav. Systems
		H. F. (prov only) ADF/LF
		VHF VOR/LOC
		UHF Glideslope
		Intercom Marker Beacon
		            TACAN
		            IFF
		            Weath. Radar

C-10A

C-10 "Extender"

Manufacturer: McDonnell-Douglas
Status: Operational
Production period/total: 1979/62 purchased, 59 in service

Serial numbers:
79-043 through 044.
Others unknown at this time.

Variants:
KC-10A: powered by three GE CF-6-50C2 turbofans.

Statistics:
Crew: 4
Cruising speed: 619 mph
Service ceiling: 33,400 feet
Range: max range 4,370 miles with max cargo, without aerial refueling

Physical characteristics:
Wingspan: 155 feet, 4 inches
Length: 181 feet, 7 inches

Height: 58 feet, 1 inch
Empty weight: 241,027 pounds
Gross weight: 590,000 pounds
Maximum payload: 164,000 pounds cargo or up to 350,000 pounds fuel.

The Story
The Air Force announced on December 19, 1977 that the McDonnell Douglas DC-10 beat out the Boeing 747 for the Advanced Tanker/Cargo Aircraft purchase. Over the course of the next several years the Air Force bought 62 of these aircraft dubbed the KC-10A Extender.

Although its primary mission is aerial refueling, the Extender combines the tasks of tanker and cargo aircraft by refueling fighters while carrying the fighters' support people and equipment during overseas deployments. The Extender can carry up to 75 people and 170,000 pounds of equipment a distance of 4,400 miles.

When maxed out for refueling, it can carry more than 350,000 pounds of fuel in its six fuel tanks–almost twice as much as the KC-135.

C-11 "Gulfstream II"

Manufacturer: Grumman
Status: Operational
Production period/total: 1970/1 bought by U.S. Coast Guard

Serial numbers:
1451, later 01 in the Executive Sequence

Variants:
None

Statistics:
Crew: 2 or 3
Cruising speed: 581 mph (max)
Service ceiling: 25,000 feet
Range: 4,123 miles

Physical characteristics:
Wingspan: 68 feet, 10 inches (without tip tanks)
Length: 79 feet, 11 inches

Height: 24 feet, 6 inches
Empty weight: 36,544 pounds
Gross weight: 65,500 pounds
Maximum payload: 2,000 pounds; 28,600 pounds with fuel (up to 19 passengers)

The Story
This single Gulfstream II was bought by the Coast Guard as an executive transport aircraft. Designated the VC-11A, it was powered by two pod-mounted Rolls-Royce Spey Mk.511-8 engines, attached to the fuselage forward of the tail.

The Gulfstream II first flew on October 2, 1966. A year later, it received its FAA certification. More than two hundred Gulfstream II's were sold during its production run, mostly to civilian customers, though a few saw military service including Cameroon, Gabon, Ivory Coast, and Nigeria.

When the Coast Guard restructured their aircraft inventory, the Gulfstream II became number 01 in the Executive transport sequence.

C-12 "Huron"

Manufacturer: Beechcraft
Status: Operational
Production period/total: 1973 through 1978/176 purchased; additional 282 ordered subsequently

Serial numbers:
73-1205 through 1219, 22250 through 22269
75-1 through 16
76-158 through 173
77-22931 through 22950
78-23126 through 23128
79- unknown

Variants:
C-12A: With two 750 horsepower turboprops. 110 were bought; 30 for USAF, the rest for the Army.
UC-12B: Navy version, with two 850 horsepower turboprops. 66 bought.

C-12C: Army aircraft re-engined with the same 850 horsepower engines the Navy uses.
C-12D: AF/Army version, same as C-12C, but with larger cargo door, high flotation landing gear and stronger wing.
RC-12D: Modified by Army to perform signal intelligence and electronic surveillance missions–mission aircraft are called Guard Rail.
C-12E: Upgraded Air Force C-12As, powered by two PT6A-42.
C-12F: Also Air Force, an operational support transport version of the commercial Super King Air B200C, 2 crew, 8 passengers.
RC-12F: UC-12F modified by the Navy, equipped with surface search radar and operators console.
UC-12F: Navy's upgraded UC-12B, with new avionics, landing gear and engines.
RC-12G: Army modification of Beech 200C, provides near real-time intelligence support to tactical commanders in the field.
RC-12H: Modified Army RC-12D, with improved signal intelligence and electronic surveillance mission capability - called Guard Rail V.
C-12J: A stretched Air Force C-12F with increased cargo/passenger capacity–up to 19 passengers. Used by the Air National Guard.

RC-12K: Army modified C-12 used to provide both communication and electronics intelligence reconnaissance.

C-12L: Army modified U-21J (Beech A100), originally purchased for the Cefly Lancer program.

RC-12M: UC-12M modified with new wings, surface search radar, mission control console–used for reconnaissance missions by the Navy.

UC-12M: Navy UC-12B and UC-12Fs modified with unique cockpit instruments, lighting and voice communication equipment.

RC-12N: Army RC-12Ks modified with improved primary mission equipment, increased payload and upgraded engines.

RC-12P: Army RC-12Ns modified with different external configurations, improved primary mission equipment, data link capability, fiber optic cabling and increase take off weight.

Statistics:
Crew: 2
Cruising speed: 275 mph
Service ceiling: 35,000 feet
Range: 1,824 miles

Physical characteristics:
Wingspan: 54 feet, 6 inches
Length: 43 feet, 9 inches
Height: 15 feet
Empty weight: 7,800 pounds
Gross weight: 12,500 pounds
Maximum payload: 2,647 pounds (8 passengers)

The Story
The Huron is a military version of the Beechcraft Super King Air A200, which first flew in October 1972. Within two years the Army had bought more than thirty for its light transport/cargo needs. About fourteen of this initial order were for Air Force use, the rest for Army purposes. The initial contract with Beech allowed for either service to exercise options for additional purchases, which both exercised. The Army added sixty, the Air Force about twenty. Also, the Navy got into the act and ordered another sixty-six for shore duty missions–no catapult launches for the Huron!

C-13 (Not Used)

Manufacturer:
Status:
Production period/total:

Serial numbers:

Variants:

Statistics:
n/a

Physical characteristics:
n/a

The Story
A short story–the government is evidently somewhat superstitious, as they skipped the -13 designation both times it has come up.

C-14 (No Nickname)

Manufacturer: Boeing
Status: Research only
Production period/total: 1972/2 built

Serial numbers:
72-1873 and 1874

Variants:
YC-14A-BN: Only designation for model.

Statistics:
Crew: 2
Cruising speed: 460 mph
Ceiling: Not reported
Range: 460 miles (STOL configuration); 2,990 miles (ferry range)

Physical Characteristics:
Wingspan: 129 feet
Length: 132 feet
Height: 48 feet
Empty weight: Not reported
Gross weight: 170,000 pounds (STOL configuration); 216,000 pounds (conventional configuration)
Maximum payload: 27,000 pounds (STOL configuration); 63,000 pounds (conventional configuration)

The Story

YC-14 was the name by which this research craft was best known, one of two entrants in the so-called Advanced Medium STOL Transport (AMST) program. The other model in the program was the McDonnell-Douglas YC-15. Both aircraft models were designed to provide a large cargo aircraft with the capability of flying in and out of extremely short, semi-prepared fields.

Two YC-14 models were produced under a $107 million contract with the Air Force. The YC-14 was built to demonstrate the feasibility of a concept called upper surface blowing (USB), in which thrust from the plane's two engines was used to blow air over the wing and flaps, thus creating powered lift.

The USB concept is based on the Coanda effect, employing the concept that high speed air will follow the surface of both a wing and its accompanying flap system if the curvative is properly designed. The wing and trailing edge flap system of the YC-14 allowed the engine exhaust air to create vertical, powered lift.

As a result, the YC-14 could take off from fields several times shorter than standard aircraft of comparable size. The plane could land on short fields at speeds as slow as 99 miles per hour.

Other new technologies on the YC-14 were an advanced flight control system and a high-floatation lever-type landing gear.

The YC-14 was powered by two General Electric CF6-50 fanjet engines, mounted near the fuselage above and at the forward edge of the wing. Each produced about 50,000 pounds of thrust.

No additional YC-14s were produced after completion of the program, but many of the developed technologies would find their way into follow-on aircraft.

YC-14

YC-15's

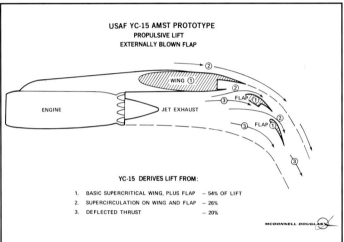

USAF YC-15 AMST PROTOTYPE
PROPULSIVE LIFT
EXTERNALLY BLOWN FLAP

WING ①
ENGINE
JET EXHAUST
FLAP ①
FLAP ①

YC-15 DERIVES LIFT FROM:

1. BASIC SUPERCRITICAL WING, PLUS FLAP — 54% OF LIFT
2. SUPERCIRCULATION ON WING AND FLAP — 26%
3. DEFLECTED THRUST — 20%

MCDONNELL DOUGLAS

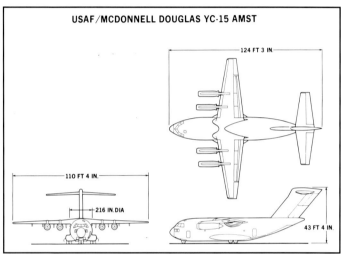

USAF/MCDONNELL DOUGLAS YC-15 AMST

124 FT 3 IN.

110 FT 4 IN.

216 IN. DIA

43 FT 4 IN.

C-15 (No Nickname)

Manufacturer: McDonnell Douglas
Status: Research only
Production period/total: Early 1972/2 built

Serial numbers:
72-1875 and 1876

Variants:
YC-15-DL: Only designation of model.

Statistics:
Crew: 2
Cruising speed: 500 mph
Ceiling: Not reported
Range: 610 miles (27,000 pound payload) (STOL); 460 miles (62,000 pound payload) (conventional mode)

Physical Characteristics:
Wingspan; 132 feet, 7 inches
Length: 124 feet, 3 inches
Height: 43 feet, 4 inches
Empty weight: Not reported

Gross weight: 216,680 pounds
Maximum payload: 62,000 pounds

The Story

The second part of the AMST program was the McDonnell Douglas C-15 transport (the first being the Boeing C-14). Two C-15 prototypes were constructed, but the program did not continue beyond the prototype stage. It should be noted, though, that the technology developed in the program would not go unused, eventually being funnelled into the C-17 advanced transport program of the 1990s. The C-15 basically served as the basis for the company's winning C-17 proposal.

Unlike the competing C-14, the C-15 used four engines–16,000 pound thrust Pratt & Whitney JT8D-17 turbofans–instead of the C-14's pair of larger engines. The engines were mounted on the wings by means of pylons that pushed the engines far forward of the wings' leading edge. The engine locations allowed the thrust to exhaust on the underside of the wing, directly into the large two-segment flaps. The engines were fitted with special nozzles to mix the hot exhaust with cool air such that no special flap material was required.

Inboard spoilers provided for the plane's lateral control and also aided in landing the craft.

There was a lot of consideration by the contractor to convert the plane for commercial use, but that possibility never materialized.

C-16 (Not Used)

Manufacturer:
Status:
Production period/total:

Serial numbers:

Variants:

Statistics:
n/a

Physical characteristics:
n/a

The Story
This designation was not allocated to any aircraft. Is it unlucky also?

C-17 "Globemaster III"

Manufacturer: McDonnell Douglas
Status: Operational
Production period/total: 1987-current/at least 40 purchased, with total buy projected to be 120.

Serial numbers:
87-0025
88-1065 and 0268
89-1189 through 1192
90-0532 through 0535
92-3291 through 3294
93-0599 through 0604
94-0065 through 0070

Variants:
C-17A: with four Pratt & Whitney F117-PW-100 engines, this is currently the only model of C-17 being produced.

Statistics:
Crew: 3
Cruising speed: 500 mph
Service ceiling: 45,000 feet
Range: without aerial refueling, with max cargo, approximately 2,600 miles, 5000+ mile ferry range. With aerial refueling, unlimited range.

Physical characteristics:
Wingspan: 169 feet, 9 inches
Length: 159 feet, 2 inches
Height: 55 feet, 2 inches
Empty weight: 265,000 pounds
Gross weight: 585,000 pounds
Maximum payload: 172,000 pounds (up to 150 passengers)

The Story
In August 1981 the Air Force selected McDonnell Douglas as the winner of the C-X competition, over entries from Boeing and Lockheed. The C-17 was designed to provide airlift capability for the full range of DOD cargo, from paratroop drops, to air-dropping vehicles, to carrying nearly every piece of hardware. The C-17 can carry M-1 Abrahms battle tanks, Apache and Blackhawk helicopters, and Patriot missile batteries.

The original plan to buy 210 airlifters was affected by drops in the defense budgets following the fall of the Soviet Union. Now the Air Force plans to buy 120 airplanes to replace the aging C-141 Starlifter.

The C-17 "Globemaster III" is the most advanced military cargo plane in history. It was also one of the most controversial. Due to a series of DOD decisions in the mid- to late 1980s, the cost of the aircraft skyrock-eted. Also, in the early 1990s the Globemaster III went through public and congressional scrutiny like no other program in history. At one point the DOD Inspector General, General Accounting Office, and the House Government Operations Committee were all reviewing the C-17 program.

During this time aircraft deliveries began, about a year behind schedule, and due to numerous factors outside the control of both the USAF and McDonnel Douglas, cost ballooned to more than $1.5 billion over budget.

Things were not going well, needless to say, when Secretary of Defense Les Aspin and Deputy SecDef John Deutch put the program on probation in December 1993. During a two-year probation period, the USAF and McDonnel Douglas had to make significant improvements in manufacturing quality, delivery schedules and reducing costs. Also, the probation included a settlement whereby the Air Force would pay MDA about $350 million in exchange for MDA dropping claims totalling more than $1.5 billion.

Also at this time, Secretary Aspin relieved from command a previous program director and forced the eventual retirement of two other general officers associated with the program over what Aspin felt were questionable progress payments to the tune of some $450 million.

The probation period ended on November 3, 1995, when Department of Defense officials announced that the Defense Acquisition Board findings supported the purchase of an additional 80 C-17s and no commercial freighters.

The political battles surrounding the program often overshadowed the incredible performance of the aircraft during testing and early operations. During flight testing, 22 world records were set, as well as other performance objectives that defy description. For instance, Congress demanded that the plane meet a contract specification for backing up a slope. Congress erroneously mandated backing up a 2 **percent** slope, not a 2 **degree** slope as was in the contract. The difference was that a 2 percent slope is approximately 3.5 degrees–nearly double the required specification. The aircraft passed with flying colors, after a long search to find a runway or ramp with this radical a slope. Picture, if you will, the C-17 at the edge of the Pentagon parking lot. It revs up its engines and begins to back up an imaginary ramp leading to the roof of the Pentagon. Mere seconds later the Globemaster has backed up the slope and is now parked on the roof of the puzzle palace.

The heart and soul of the Globemaster III (who thinks of these names?) is in the back half of the plane. The cargo hold is designed to hold nearly every piece of DOD equipment, and to airdrop nearly all of them.

Designed to operate out of short, austere airfields, the C-17 uses a propulsive lift system which uses exhaust gases to generate lift. By directing the engine exhaust over large flaps extended into the exhaust stream, the aircraft can fly steep approaches at relatively slow landing speeds, resulting in safe, short landings.

The only airlifter equipped with both a Heads Up Display–a HUD–and a control stick, not a yoke, the C-17 flies very much like a very large, squatty fighter. Having personally flown on a C-17 at 300 mph at 300 feet, I greatly appreciated this handling capability!

C-18 Airborne Range Instrumentation Aircraft (ARIA)

Manufacturer: Boeing
Status: Research only
Production period/total: Various models modified

Serial numbers:
unidentified

Variations:
C-18A: Modified commercial Boeing 707.
C-18B: Modified for MILSTAR mission.
EC-18B: ARIA modification.
EC-18C: J-STAR modifications.
EC-18D: Cruise missile modifications.
TC-18E: E3 pilot training.

Statistics:
Crew: Depends on particular research mission
Cruising speed: Depends on mission configuration
Ceiling: Depends on mission configuration
Range: Depends on mission configuration

Physical characteristics:
Wingspan: Approximately 142 feet
Length: Approximately 153 feet
Height: Approximately 49 feet

Empty weight: Depends on mission configuration
Gross weight: Depends on mission configuration
Maximum payload: Depends on mission configuration

The Story
The C-18 (basically a Boeing commercial 707 model) proved to be a great configuration for modification to various testbeds. Through the years, the model has received modifications to support MILSTAR, ARIA, J-STAR, E-3 pilot training, and cruise missile tracking missions.

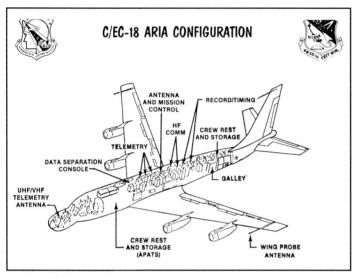

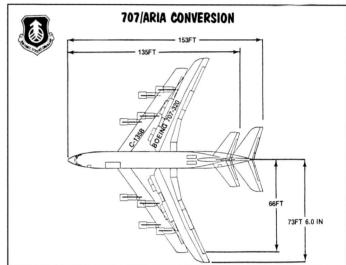

C-19 (No Nickname)

Manufacturer: Boeing
Status: Operational
Production period/total: 1985-1990/19 modified 747s

Serial numbers:
No military serial numbers

Variants:
C-19A: Modified 747s.

Statistics: Boeing 747
Crew: 3
Cruising speed: 580 mph
Service ceiling: 40,000 feet
Range: 5,000+ miles

Physical characteristics:
Wingspan: 195 feet, 8 inches
Length: 231 feet, 10 inches
Height: 63 feet, 5 inches
Empty weight: unknown

Gross weight: 825,000 pounds
Maximum payload: not reported

The Story
The USAF modified nineteen PanAm 747s for Civil Reserve Air Force (CRAF) use. CRAF used to supplement military transport forces by providing airlift of bulk and oversize cargo during emergencies.

The main deck was strengthened, along with the installation of a cargo handling system and side cargo door. The empty weight was increased by 13,000 pounds. Planes are used in all pax mode by Pan Am (and others) until called for by the Secretary of Defense. Then they become USAF aircraft and seats are removed.

Because of the extra weight added during the modifications, government offsets the extra fuel burn rates by paying the carrier an amount equal to pre-modification burn rates.

C-20 "Gulfstream"

Manufacturer: Gulfstream Aerospace
Status: Operational
Production period/total: 1980s/approximately 18 bought

Serial Numbers:
Unknown

Variants:
C-20A: First Air Force version (Gulfstream III).
C-20B: Air Force variation (Gulfstream III).
C-20C: Air Force One back-up plan (Gulfstream III).
C-20D: First Navy version (Gulfstream III).
C-20E: First Army version (Gulfstream IV).
C-20F: First Army version (Gulfstream IV).
C-20G: Navy version (Gulfstream IV).
C-20H: Air Force version (Gulfstream IV).
C-20J: Army version (Gulfstream IV).
Tp 102: Swedish Designation.
No military designation: New Gulfstream V model.

Statistics:
Crew: 5
Cruising speed: 561 mph
Ceiling: 45,000 feet
Range: 4,050 miles

Physical Characteristics:
Wingspan: 77 feet, 10 inches
Length: 83 feet, 11 inches
Height: 24 feet, 4 inches
Empty weight: 35,000 pounds
Gross weight: 69,700 pounds
Maximum payload: Not reported (14 passengers)

The Story
The C-20 has proved to be one of the best short-range jet transports ever ordered by the Air Force. The Air Force had originally planned on buying eight of the planes over a three year time period (three in 1986, three in 1987, and two in 1988). But in order to save $50 million, the complete purchase was made in 1986.

There would be later deliveries of the model, including a C-20F version to the U.S. Army Davison Air Command at Andrews Air Force Base in 1991, and four C-20G to the U.S. Navy and one to the USMC in 1994. Finally, there was a single C-20H delivered to the USAF in 1994.

Through the years, the planes would be modified to fulfill a number of unique mission requirements, including electronic warfare support, electronic surveillance/reconnaissance, and anti-submarine warfare missions.

The Swedish Air Force ordered three of the models under the Tp 102 designation. Two of the planes would be modified for reconnaissance duties.

At the time of printing, there also was a Gulfstream V under development, but no military orders had yet been made for the improved model.

C-21 (No Nickname)

Manufacturer: Learjet
Status: Operational
Production period/total: 1984-1986/84 ordered; 1991/4 more ordered

Serial Numbers:
Not available

Variants:
C-21A: Only designation given to model.

Statistics:
Crew: 2
Cruising speed: 530 mph
Ceiling: 41,000 feet
Range: 2,300 miles

Physical characteristics:
Wingspan: 39 feet, 6 inches
Length: 48 feet, 7 inches

Height: 12 feet, 3 inches
Empty weight: 10,120 pounds
Gross weight: 18,300 pounds
Maximum payload: 3,380 pounds (8 passengers)

The Story
The Learjet C-21A was the right plane for the right job. Delivery of the fleet occurred during the 1984-1985 time period and many of the planes were still in service a decade later. There were actually two company designations for the model, the 35A and 35B, which differed in fuel capacity and accommodations.

The configuration featured fuselage-mounted turbofan engines quite far forward. The sleek machine featured swept-back wings and hydraulically actuated single-slotted flaps. There also is a tricycle landing gear.

The initial order for the C-21 was for eighty of the model, followed by four ordered for the Air National Guard in 1987. The final order came in 1991 for four special mission versions.

C-22 (No Nickname) Production Logo

Manufacturer: Boeing
Status: Operational
Production period/total: 1963/4 produced

Serial numbers:
Not available

Variants:
C-22B: Designation of operational version.

Statistics:
Crew: 7 or 8
Cruising speed: 619 mph
Ceiling: Not available
Range: 2,000 miles

Physical Characteristics:
Wingspan: 108 feet
Length: 133 feet, 2 inches
Height: 34 feet
Empty weight: Not available
Gross weight: 170,000 pounds
Maximum payload: 20,000 pounds

The Story
The C-22B is an example of the Air Force taking a commercial development directly into military service. Of course, in the case of this plane, the starting point was the Boeing 727 transport. Only four were purchased, all used by the 201st Airlift Squadron of the District of Columbia Air National Guard.

The plane was revolutionary in that its unique arrangement of leading edge devices and flaps allowed the use of lower approach speeds and shorter runway operation.

The twin aft-mounted engines (JT8D-7 engines) were mounted horizontally-opposed on the rear fuselage and produced 14,000 pounds of thrust each.

In the mid-1990s, another C-22-type designation came on the scene in the form of the CV-22 trimotor research aircraft. The plane, which was fashioned after the V-22, was capable of taking off and landing like a helicopter, but flew like a traditional aircraft once aloft.

The final status of this "other C-22" remained clouded at press time.

C-23 "Sherpa" Production Logo

Manufacturer: Short Brothers
Status: Operational
Production period/total: Early 1980s/18 ordered

Serial numbers:
Not available

Variants:
C-23A: Only designation of the model.

Statistics:
Crew: 3
Cruising speed: 157 mph
Ceiling: At least 10,000 feet
Range: 406 miles (with 4,200 pounds)

Physical Characteristics:
Wingspan: 74 feet, 8 inches
Length: 58 feet
Height: 16 feet, 3 inches
Empty weight: Not reported
Gross weight: 25,500 pounds
Maximum payload: 7,000 pounds (freight only)

The Story
Quite simply, there was a need for an aircraft like this one, to move around the some six thousand line items to USAF units in Europe. The C-23 definitely filled the need. There was no need to develop a new aircraft for the European supply mission; the plane was already in existence with the Short Sherpa aircraft. With the C-23A's cabin dimensions of 30 x 6.5 x 6.5 feet, this was the plane for the job.

The C-23A also has the unique capability of being able to take off and land within a 2,000 foot envelope, far superior to the larger transport planes such as the C-141 and C-5. The plane also has a very flexible rear-loading ramp door.

Power is provided by a pair of Pratt & Whitney Canada PT6A-45R turboprops, each producing 1,198 horsepower.

The Air Force took its first delivery in 1984 and the concept has proved to be very effective, exactly the way it was planned. The plane is not what you would call sleek or aerodynamic, but it doesn't matter. With its slow speed and dependability, it provides overnight delivery service that kept the Air Force in Europe in a high state of readiness.

The C-23As were later transferred back to the United States, where they were assigned to the Air Force (as chase planes at Edwards AFB in California), to the Army, and to the U.S. Forest Service.

C-24 (No Nickname)

Manufacturer: Douglas
Status: Simulator
Production period/total: 1 modification

Serial numbers:
Unknown

Variants:
EC-24: Only designation of model.

Statistics:
Unknown

Physical Characteristics:
Unknown

The Story
The only data available on the 'C' plane that carries this designation is that it is a former United DC-8 548 freighter that was modified by the Navy to simulate a C3 threat.

C-25 "Air Force One"

Manufacturer: Boeing
Status: Operational
Production period/total: Late 1980s, early 1990s/2 procured

Serial numbers:
(Years not reported) 28000, 29000
Variants:
VC-25A: Only designation of the model.

Statistics:
Crew: 26
Cruising speed: 701 mph
Ceiling: 45,100 feet
Range: 9,600 miles

Physical Characteristics:
Wingspan: 195 feet, 8 inches
Length: 231 feet, 10 inches
Height: 63 feet, 5 inches
Empty weight: Not reported
Gross weight: 833,000 pounds
Maximum payload: Not reported (102 total crew and passengers)

The Story
In the late 1980s, it was time for a new 'Air Force One' Presidential aircraft and the decision was made to use the existing Boeing 747 for the mission.

The first of the two planes joined the fleet in 1990 with the second following in 1991. The new planes replaced the longstanding Boeing 727-320C that had served the function for about three decades.

Not surprisingly, the new Air Force One has greatly enhanced communications capability. It also shows a 35 percent greater range and a runway requirement considerably less than the other planes in the Presidential fleet.

The plane has seats for staff, press and the Secret Service as the President carries his large family around the country and world. There is also a full galley and sleeping quarters for the President and first lady. With its huge space, the President can conduct business just as if he were at home in the White House.

The planes are powered by four General Electric CF6-80C21B1 powerplants (56,000 pounds of thrust each) and are operated by the 89th Airlift Wing at Andrews Air Force Base.

The SN28000 Air Force One first flew in September 1990 when it transported President Bush to Florida and back. The second Air Force One was first deployed in March 1991.

C-26 (No Nickname)

Manufacturer: Fairchild
Status: Operational
Production period/total: 1980 through 1997/at least 43 bought

Serial numbers:
unavailable

Variants:
C-26A: 13 ordered by USAF Air National Guard Operational Support Transport Aircraft (ANGOSTA), with quick-change interiors–from medevac to cargo to passengers.
C-26B: 30 ordered, 23 options for AF and Army Guard units. First delivered to 12 TFW, Truax Field, Wisconsin.

Statistics:
Crew: 2
Cruising speed: 358 mph (max.)
Service ceiling: 27,500 feet
Range: 1,324 miles (max. fuel)

Physical characteristics:
Wingspan: 57 feet
Length: 59 feet, 4 inches
Height: 16 feet, 8 inches
Empty weight: 9,180 pounds
Gross weight: 16,500 pounds
Maximum payload: 5,000 pounds (19 or 20 passengers)

The Story
The C-26 is a militarized version of Fairchild's Metro III, a commuter aircraft. The C-26 Mission Support Aircraft (MSA) is operated by the National Guards of both the Air Force and the Army, replacing the aging C-131 aircraft.

The C-26B was the first military aircraft to be qualified with a Traffic Alert Collision Avoidance System II and a commercial Global Positioning System. Also, when it was introduced it was one of only two aircraft (the other being the VC-25A–Air Force One) with a certified microwave landing system which allows landings in virtually zero ceiling/zero visibility conditions.

C-27 "Spartan"

Manufacturer: Alenia (Italy)
Status: Operational
Production period/total: 1990-91/10 bought

Serial numbers:
unknown

Variants:
C-27A: Powered by two Fiat-built GE T64-GE-P4D turbo props.

Statistics:
Crew: 3
Cruising speed: 273 mph
Service ceiling: 25,000 feet
Range: 852 miles (max. weight), 2879 (ferry)

Physical characteristics:
Wingspan: 94 feet, 2 inches
Length: 74 feet, 5 inches
Height: 32 feet, 2 inches
Empty weight: 32,165 pounds
Gross weight: 61,730 pounds
Maximum payload: 19,840 pounds (53 passengers max.)

The Story
Bought by the USAF, the 10 Spartans are used for transport missions in Panama and South America. The aircraft were bought "off the shelf" from Alenia, company model G222-710, and modified for Air Force use by Chrysler Technologies Airborne Systems.

C-28 "No Nickname"

Manufacturer: Cessna
Status: operational
Production period/total: unknown

Serial numbers: unknown

Variants: unknown

Statistics: unknown

Physical characteristics: unknown

The Story
This Cessna model 404 is used by the Navy for transporting personnel. There is very little information in the military channels regarding this C-28, but the civilian version can carry eight to ten passengers and some cargo.

C-29 (No Nickname)

Manufacturer: LTV awarded contract, planes are British Aerospace
Status: Operational
Production period/total: 1980s/6 bought

Serial numbers:
unavailable

Variants:
C-29A: Only designation for this model.

Statistics:
Crew: 2
Cruising speed: 461 mph
Service ceiling: 43,000 feet
Range: 3,454 miles

Physical characteristics:
Wingspan: 51 feet, 4 inches
Length: 51 feet, 2 inches

Height: 17 feet, 7 inches
Empty weight: 14,720 pounds
Gross weight: 27,400 pounds
Maximum payload: 2,400 pounds

The Story
The C-29A contract was awarded to LTV Missiles and Electronics Group, Buffalo, NY, but the aircraft are versions of the British Aerospace BAe 125-800, a twin engine jet.

The six C-29A are used for worldwide flight inspection and ground navigation calibration.

During crises and other quick reaction situations, these aircraft are used to establish ground navigational and air traffic control systems, or check to see if current ones are operating properly, before the others can bring in troops or equipment.

They also are used to calibrate Instrument Landing System (ILS) equipment at bases worldwide. The ILS is a system of radars and specialized onboard equipment that allows aircraft to land in adverse weather.

The C-29A's are stationed at Scott AFB, IL; Ramstein AB, Germany; and Yokota AB, Japan.

C-30 "No Nickname"

Manufacturer: none
Status: none
Production period/total: n/a

Serial numbers: n/a

Variants: n/a

Statistics: n/a

Physical characteristics: n/a

The Story
Evidently this number also was skipped for reasons unknown.

C-31

Manufacturer: Fokker
Status: Operational
Production period/total: 1980s/1 purchased

Serial numbers:
unknown

Variants:
C-31A: Only designation for this aircraft.

Statistics:
Crew: 2
Cruising speed: 298 mph
Service ceiling: 30,000 feet
Range: 1,197 miles

Physical characteristics:
Wingspan: 95 feet, 2 inches
Length: 77 feet, 3 inches
Height: 9 feet, 1 inches
Empty weight: 25,500 pounds
Gross weight: 45,900 pounds
Maximum payload: 14,000 pounds (44 passengers)

The Story
The C-31 was bought and is used for support of the Golden Knights. The Knights are the U.S. Army parachute demonstration team. The appear at airshows around the world, showing off their skills and acting as a recruiting tool for the Army.

VC-32

Manufacturer: none yet determined
Status: negotiation
Production period/total: n/a

Serial numbers: n/a

Variants: n/a

Statistics:
none

Physical characteristics:
none

The Story

The VC-32 is the planned replacement for the VC-137, the aging executive transports used by the vice president and other government leaders.

The VC-137 does not meet the new FAA noise and emission standards, but bringing it up to FAA standards would be prohibitively expensive. The decision was made to begin acquiring a replacement aircraft, the VC-32, with a lease-to-buy clause. Since money to buy new planes would not be in the Air Force budget until 1997, permission was received from the Chief of Staff to use the money that would have paid for the engine upgrades and modifications to lease up to six aircraft. When the acquisition money is available in 1997, that money will be used to purchase the jets.

The Request for Proposal was issued by the Air Force in the spring of 1995, and a decision is expected shortly.

C-33 "Non Developmental Airlift Aircraft"

Manufacturer: Unknown at press time, but most likely Boeing, with MacDonnell Douglas a possibility
Status: none
Production period/total: n/a

Serial numbers: none

Variants: none

Statistics: n/a

Physical characteristics: n/a

The Story

The C-33 designation was assigned to what was to have a commercial freighter that would augment the C-17 aircraft. That program, called NDAA, piqued the interest of a number of aircraft manufacturers and suppliers. The initial Request For Proposal drew 11 entries from U.S., European and Russian companies. Eventually, the field narrowed down to two legitimate contenders. Boeing was pushing the 747-400F hard and was considered a near lock for a contract of at least 20 aircraft. The other contender, though with little real chance of winning a contract, was Lockheed with a C-5D version.

On November 3, 1995, the Defense Acquisition Board decided that the C-17 was back on schedule (actually ahead of schedule) with high manufacturing quality and costs were coming down.

In a commendable instance of providing the military leaders with what they needed and wanted, not what is politically correct, the DAB decided to forego buying any C-33 aircraft.

Just days before the DAB meeting convened on Halloween, every member of the Joint Chiefs of Staff and the warfighting commands signed a letter to the board recommending a full C-17 purchase and not C-33 purchases. Their voices were heard.

It is not known at publication time whether or not this designation will be recycled like the C-10 designation in the early 1980s.